EMPOWERING
MOTHERS TO MOTHER

Winnie Kitaka

ACKNOWLEDGEMENTS

Being a youth leader in my local church, I was a mentor and coach for many young people. During this time I worked with the women's department, visiting and helping mothers during the first few weeks of giving birth. Seven years ago, I gave birth to my first baby, a son, Master Divine Kitaka. Like his name, he was divine from day one and he slept from 8pm to 8am. I wondered what other mothers meant by sleepless nights; in my personal experience at that time; I enjoyed being a mother as I had enough sleep every night.

Two years down the line I gave birth to Dorrinda Kitaka, and one year later, Debra Kitaka was born. Danielle Kitaka was born 18th December 2013. It is during this season of my life that I appreciated my mother more than I ever did before. Dorrinda woke up every two hours at night; I had a three year old, twelve months-old and a newborn baby, and being constantly sleep deprived, even the simplest tasks seemed like climbing a mountain carrying all three children on my back. I remember one such night with tears streaming down my face, praying and vowing, "if I can help another mother get a few hours of sleep I will." This is why I have written this book.

I have worked with mothers for more than ten years now, and during this time I learned that all mothers, regardless of their social standing, profession, culture, and country of residence, have similar challenges. The one I encounter most frequently is mothers feeling guilty. In writing this book, I want to thank these mothers for allowing me into their homes and their babies' lives; my children, without whom I would not be a mother, my own mother for raising a strong woman, and my husband, Francis Kitaka for being a wonderful father.

I would also like to thank my mother, Christine Kiyimba and my younger sister, Maria Kabuye for always being there to help with the children. My brothers, Ronald Kiyimba and Richard Kiyimba for being brilliant uncles to my children. My sisters, Margaret Mugema and Solome Masembe, you are wonderful mothers. Thank you to Prossy, a wonderful maternity nurse who mentored me as a maternity nurse. Thank you to *Night Nannies* for introducing me to countless mothers. I spent close to a year talking to Claire Ferrini on the phone and I finally met her after the birth of her third baby; thank you for all your support.

Finally, thank you to Geoffrey Semaganda (Action Wealth Publishing). I am truly grateful for the countless hours working on this book, as he has been on call as a mentor and coach, and he remains that always.

Thank you also, Readers, for choosing "Empowering Mothers'.

TABLE OF CONTENTS

Introduction

"What do you really want to do?"

I, like so many other young people, wasn't exactly sure what I wanted to do with my life. I'd been to Greenwich University and majored in International Marketing. After leaving school, I was approached by a non-profit foundation and was invited to become a part of the team, as Event Coordinator their premier fundraising event, a concert at the Barbican London.

I worked there for two years, and then ended up at the HM. Treasury as a Personal Assistant. I got on well with my boss at the Treasury, Ray. I looked to him like a father. He was invested in my success and wanted me to do well. We were talking one day and he asked me, "What do you really want to do? Just tell me, what is it that you want to do?"

I said, "You know what I want to do? I want to be a voice for somebody. I want to be a voice for something. I want to speak up for those who can't speak up for themselves. All I know is I want to be a voice. I can't tell you whether it's this or it's that, but I just want to be a voice, I want to be able to speak out for people that maybe can't speak up for themselves." We talked about a couple of different ideas, and that conversation always stayed with me.

Eventually, I went on to get married and have kids. During my pregnancies and subsequent maternity leaves, I always tried to add value to myself. I asked, *what can I do during these nine months that would help me add value to me and to what I'm doing?* After my second baby, I had planned on going back to work as a personal assistant, but it was not appealing. I knew it wasn't my passion and it quickly became apparent that nine-to-five work was not my cup of tea. I looked back at my conversation with Ray and knew that I had to make some changes.

I found a lady who was training a group at my local church to become maternity nurses. The lady teaching the class needed a baby as a model to allow the students to practice how to bathe a baby. I volunteered. As I watched them trying to bathe my baby and listened to what they were doing, I thought, *I could do that.*

The teacher told me that she thought I was perfect for the job. She said, "I will help you, I will train you." My initial thought was, *looking after babies? I don't think so. I've got my own baby.* But she said, "Honestly, trust me, you will be the perfect person for this job." I decided to give it a try, came up with some money, and within about a month, I had finished the training. I was placed in a job and started working almost immediately.

As it turns out, she was right. I had found the perfect job for me. I was able to combine my experience as a mother with my training and my desire to be a voice for someone.

Out of every 100 women who give birth, 10 to 15 of them experience post partum depression. Countless others experience the universal uncertainty and anxiety that comes with being a new parent. Many don't receive the support they need and end up feeling inadequate and stressed.

What I learned very quickly as a maternity nurse is these women had forgotten a fundamental thing about being a mother – *they already know how to do it.* They know their baby best. Nature has given them everything they need to care for and love their baby. But too much noise from the outside world, a lack of support, and their own insecurities cause them to question their ability as a mother.

It became my goal to show these women that not only were they capable of taking care of their babies – they were capable of being *great* mothers. I wanted to show them that it was okay to ask for help when they needed it and to stand up for their needs and the needs of their baby.

I believe in empowering mothers. In being a source of support, encouragement, and information. When I'm working with a mother, sometimes all it takes is for me to say, "I'm a mother too. This is normal. You can do this." With those simple words, this woman feels back on top, because she understands that what she's feeling is not isolated to her. She isn't the only one. She's not a bad mum because she feels this way.

My goal in writing this book is not only to share some of what I've learned as a maternity nurse, but also to arm new mothers with a reference that will help them through the early days of being a new mum.

We are all bound together by the stress and profound joy of being a mother. It's my goal to bring us all together, to provide support, encouragement, and above all, understanding to each other.

Chapter 1

We Are Our Own Worst Enemy

With my first child, I remember feeling a combination of totally contradictory feelings; joy and sadness, peace and anxiety, strength and weakness. One day I would be on top of the world, in complete awe that I was able to care for this little life and the next I would be convinced that I had no idea what I was doing and somebody should come and take this baby away from me before I really messed something up. It was confusing, to say the least.

Working as a maternity nurse gives me the opportunity to be in people's homes during almost any time of the day and witness new mums dealing with these same emotions. However, I typically work evenings so I can be home during the day with my own children. I arrive at 9pm and stay with the family until 7am. This has allowed me to have a unique vantage point to a new mum's most common struggle: feeling overwhelmed.

I'm basically there as a helper to mum. If she's breastfeeding, I go get the baby, bring him to mum, when he's done eating, I wind him, do a nappy change, and then put him back to bed. If mum is bottle feeding, I help wash the bottles and put the baby to sleep. Once the mother goes to sleep, I stay in the same room as the baby. If the baby wakes up in the middle of the night, I bring him to mum, take care of basic needs like nappy changing and whatever else needs to be done so that the night goes smoothly for mum and baby.

The longer I worked as a maternity nurse, the more I realized that my job was much more than taking care of a baby's simple needs. I was there for the mother as a source of information, support, and help, but above all, I was there to encourage. Over and over, mums would tell me that there was some kind of medical reason that their baby wouldn't feed or sleep. And in some cases, that was true; reflux, being tongue-tied, and other medical issues can all affect a baby's ability to feed and sleep. But more often than not, I would find there was nothing wrong with the baby. But the mums would *insist* that there was something going on, saying "My baby just won't feed."

In the absence of a diagnosed medical problem, I always say to the parent, "I'll come in for the first day to assess the situation." So I go in, feed the baby, and inevitably, the baby feeds. So I say to mum, "No, the baby is feeding properly. There's no problem." I always advise them to double check with their doctor or midwife, but there is almost always nothing medically wrong with the baby.

So what *is* the problem? To be blunt – it's the mum. She may be struggling with the baby blues, the stress of no sleep, a lack of support, or feeling isolated, but all of her doubt and anxiety makes it difficult for her to relax and feed the baby – and babies feel stress. Then they don't feed well.

So what's causing all the stress? It is a combination – a perfect storm, really – of factors that contribute to new mothers feeling isolated and alone in their confusing feelings. Unfortunately, most new mums don't feel like they can talk about their negative emotions. They feel that if they don't only express the joy and love they're experiencing, people will think they're a bad mum. So no one talks openly about it. The result is that new mums who experience these totally normal emotions end up feeling isolated and as though they must be the only woman in the world who doesn't love taking care of her baby 100% of the time.

Competition

There is a deep desire in today's society to "keep up with the Joneses". We are constantly comparing our experiences, our house, our clothes, our looks, and on and on, to everyone around us. New mums are no different. They're always in competition with one another, so they're always trying to make sure they look better than Mrs. A or Mrs. B.

Many times they are in competition with their own friends. Interestingly, I have found that I've never met a group of people that lie more than mothers. I don't know why, but they lie and lie and lie. They have a compulsion to out-do one another and impress each other with all the amazing things their babies can do, how easy it's been for them, how quickly they lost the baby weight, etc.

So now you have a mum who's just had a baby. She's used to being a size 10, looking fantastic. Right now, she's not looking her best. She wants to breastfeed, but she still wants to eat a grape a day so she drops the weight fast. She thinks, *I don't think my husband likes me because now I've had the baby, and maybe I don't look so good. Why does Karen's baby already sleep through the night? Why can her baby play the piano and mine can't?*

So she keeps all her doubts to herself – she says nothing and continues to think she's a terrible mother. She is constantly stressed out.

Information Overload

In this day and age, almost anything we want is right at our fingertips. With the internet and smart phones, we can have most of our questions answered immediately. Unfortunately, there is *too* much information. Not only does searching for a certain problem reveal so many options that you would never be able to read through them all, but it also reveals the very *worst* scenarios. Googling something as simple as "baby not sleeping" will reveal everything: from helpful hints to criticisms about certain ways of parenting, to horror stories about SIDS (Sudden Infant Death Syndrome).

Information is great, but for mothers, it's become one of the biggest reasons why they're so depressed because there's just so much information. You can go to YouTube, you can go to Google, and you can ask friends on Facebook. There's going to be tons and tons of information, people who say, "I've tried this one, and I've tried that one, and I've tried this one," but nothing seems to work for you. It's almost impossible to pick out one solution and say, okay, this one will work for me. The end result is that mothers feel *more* overwhelmed and inadequate.

Isolation

Having a new baby is hard work. With the lack of a schedule (and sleep!) leaving the house can be hard, if not impossible. Friends and family may be scared to bother you, so they don't visit or call much. Your spouse is adjusting and may be nervous to handle the baby – or if you're breastfeeding, simply may not be able to help as much as you'd like. All of this can leave new mums feeling isolated and alone. They're doing most of the work and they don't feel like they can admit that this is just plain hard.

Societal Expectations

In recent years a media phenomenon known as "mommy wars" has broken out between working mums and stay at home mums. Each side attempts to convince the other that their family's lifestyle is somehow harmful to their children. It's a subject many women are understandably passionate about. After all, we all want what is best for our families.

Unfortunately, this tension only makes mothers feel bad about their choices. Since the beginning of time, mothers are expected to be nurturing, to harbour a desire to take care of their babies, and make sacrifices to do so. But modern day women are faced with the challenge of balancing their personal and professional life. Some of us have to work in order to support our household. Some of us simply *like* to work. Some of us would like – and are able to – stay at home with our children.

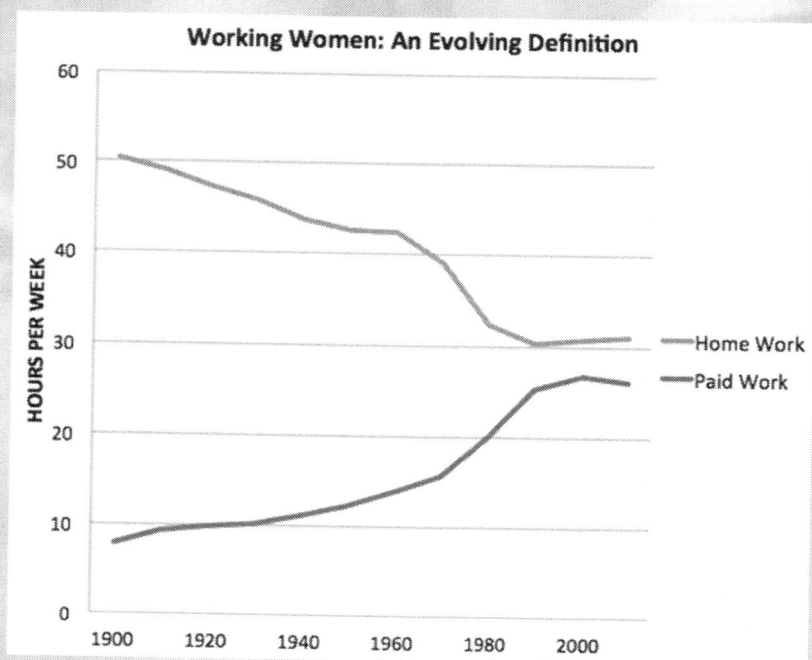

Working Women: An Evolving Definition

The following chart, from a June 2013 article on www. theatlantic.com, illustrates the extreme shift women have made in the last century from being caregivers stationed primarily at home, to women working and earning a wage outside of the home.

Whatever your situation, it's important that you don't let anyone else try to tell you that what you're doing is wrong or that another way would be better. Your family situation is unique – and you're doing what is best for your children.

The Result

The combined effects of competition, too much information, and isolation, results in mums who are too hard on themselves and expect too much from themselves. Mums have to eat so they produce enough milk to feed their baby. They have to be able to talk about their feelings so they know they're not the only mum who ever felt overwhelmed by being a mum. They have to have trusted sources of information that will help them while also providing support.

New mums lose sight of the fact that the baby is fine. In the first few weeks of life, babies eat and sleep and poo – if you give the baby their food, change their nappy, put them to sleep – the baby is fine. But all of this other noise prevents them from seeing this clearly.

So often, I sit mums down and simply ask how they're doing. The result is a floodgate of emotions:

> "I'm depressed and can't produce the milk that I need to breastfeed the baby."

> "I feel like a terrible mother because I just want a break from the baby."

> "I'm not good at this."

> "Why do I feel so bad?"

> "None of my friends with babies say that they're struggling. I must be a terrible mum."

They can't really tell their friends about it. They can't even tell their husbands about it because he might think she's not the woman he married anymore. They have all this going on in their heads.

Often, the only people new mums feel comfortable reaching out to are medical professionals. After all, they should be objective and supportive, right? But there is a pervasive attitude today that all new mums are depressed. So if a woman asks her doctor, she will probably be prescribed medication, which may help for a little while, but in the end, it doesn't address the root of the problem; these new mums don't realize their own potential and role as their baby's perfect caretaker.

When I had my babies, health visitors visited me. And it always felt as though those people were reading from a script. They work under the assumption that all women are like this and don't take into account what *you're* like.

I believe that many medical professionals are afraid to go off script. If you offer something other than the "standard" advice, you run the risk of legal trouble. If you let a mother just do what she thought was best, give her a chance to do the right thing, just be with the child, you might be held responsible if something went wrong.

But I don't believe that. Hence why empowering the mothers themselves to take responsibility is actually the most important solution. They will take ownership of doing what is right.

So I say, "I'm a mother too. All the things you're feeling, it's normal. We all feel the same way, whether you're rich, whether you're poor, whether you live in London, whether you live in Manchester, everybody feels the same way."

I remember one mother I was working with. She would just sit on the kitchen floor and say, "No, I'm not even sitting on the chair." She would sit on the kitchen floor, and it would be like she was coming to counselling. She would talk and talk. I just let her, because I knew she didn't have anybody else. She was lying to her friends because she was trying to keep up the persona that she was this perfect woman, and everything was perfect in her world. But she was obviously not okay.

The relief on her face as she talked was palpable. I find that most of the time all these women need is some encouragement – somebody to empower them and say, "You can do this".

I realized that apart from just being a night nanny taking care of their babies, that I had a chance to be their voice – to empower them to take care of their babies and believe in themselves. I had found my purpose – to help other mothers.

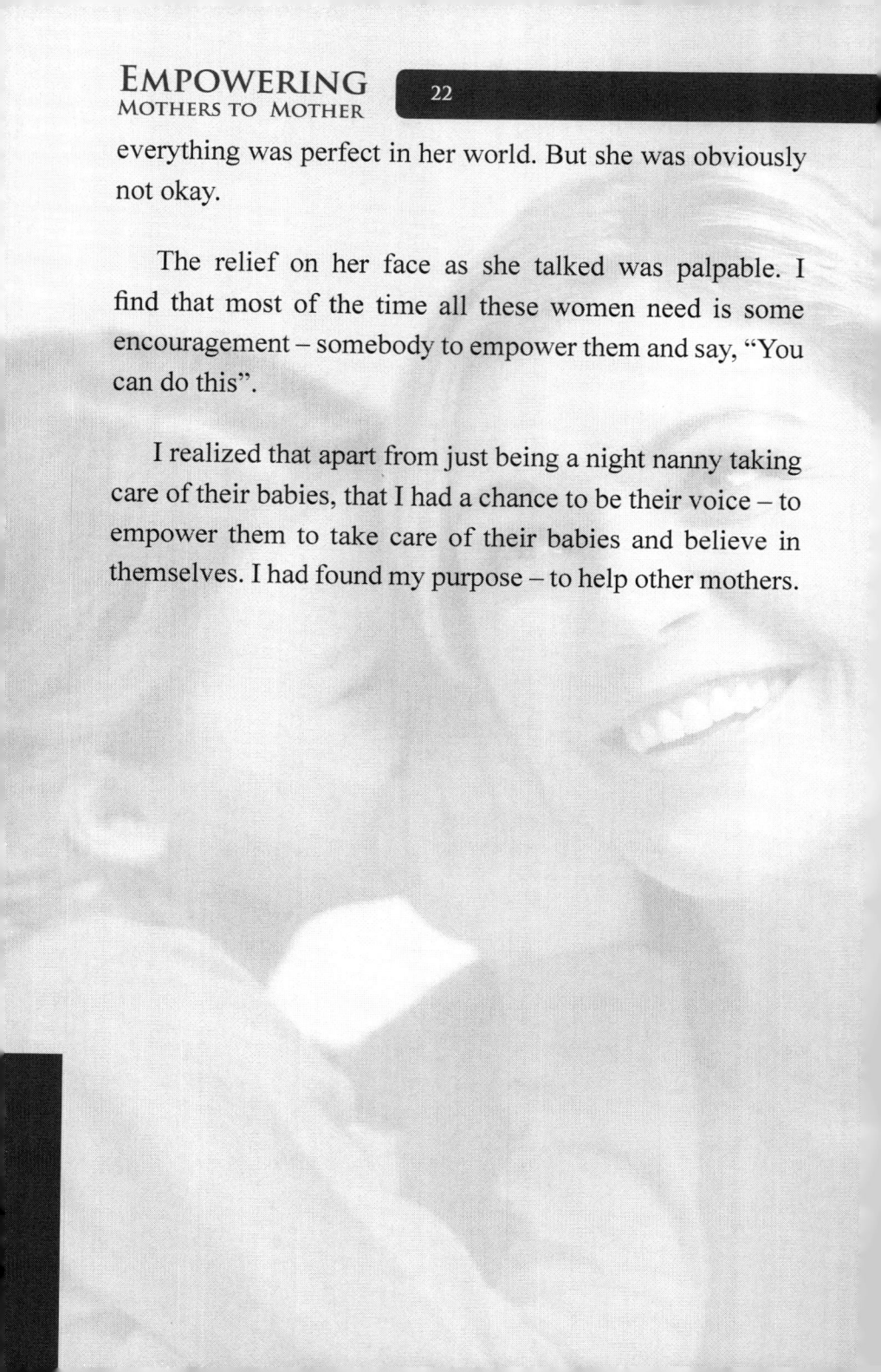

Chapter 2

The Importance of Empowerment

Like falling in love or going to war, being a parent is something that you can't truly understand until it happens to you. As a night nanny, I often find that women don't really open up to me until I tell them I'm a mother. As soon as I tell them that, they drop their guard. They know that I understand what they're going through.

Getting these women to talk causes an amazing transformation. They go from crying and questioning their capability as a parent to opening up, admitting it is hard, and eventually realizing that they can handle it. Most of the time, within a few days, they are feeling back on top. Not because I've given some magical advice or fixed all their problems. All I've done is helped them to understand that what they're feeling is not isolated to themselves. It doesn't mean they are the only one or that they are bad mums because they're feeling this way.

I went through it, and millions of other mothers have gone through it. It's normal. And you can take care of your baby. Baby will be fine.

Mums are the most important people on the planet. Think of all the ways – good and bad – that your mother has influenced you. When we empower mums – to trust themselves and do what they know is right for their baby – amazing things happen.

Unfortunately, in many cultures, there is a pervasive belief that you can't break a cycle – whether it's a cycle of abuse, or allowing your children to be parented by nannies, or of simply not being a hands-on, confident parent. Many of us parent the way our parents did, without ever considering that things could be different for our own children.

It's so sad because I believe the reason why some of the children and even the adults are now the way they are is because they were raised by somebody who did not know how to be a parent.

I want to break that. If the mums of my generation could be empowered to raise our kids the right way then that means our kids are going to have role models to look up to.

When something happens with one of my kids that I'm not sure how to handle, I think back to what my mum did. And if what my mum did was good, then fantastic, I'm going to do that. Then my kids will copy me when they run into the same difficult situation with their kids.

But what if what their mum did was a bad thing? This is going to be carried through generationally, and it's going to continue and continue. I've seen it over and over again.

To a certain degree, it's ignorance. Not in a bad sense, but some people just don't know. Somebody needs to come in now and break this struggle.

My passion is to be able to come in, even if it's to start with one woman, and say, "Look, you can be a good mum. Maybe your mum didn't do so well, but you can be a good mum".

I like to use this analogy: Babies are like a blank piece of paper. When they come into the world, they're blank, and you, as their mum, get to write onto this blank piece of paper. So what are you writing onto your baby's blank piece of paper when you're screaming and stressing and not trusting yourself?

Babies pick up on stress. I guarantee you if a baby is not sleeping, and they're agitated, the mum's stressed. If the mum's stressed, the baby's going to be stressed. Many times, I go in and the mum will almost look at me in tears, "I don't understand." Literally, I'll walk in through the door, the baby's screaming, and the parents are like, "For goodness sake, can someone just make this baby just be quiet?"

I come in, I pick the baby up and say "There you go, baby, how you doing?" And almost immediately, the baby's calm, and then they say to me, "Okay. You need to tell us exactly what it is you just did there to make that baby stop screaming," and I say, "All in good time. You need to understand that everything you do, your baby picks up on."

If you have insecure, depressed, and isolated mums – who aren't that way because they want to be, but because of the circumstances of the environments they're in – that means you're going to raise babies who are going to be exactly that way.

I believe there's a way of stopping that – empowering mums. When you empower mothers, the benefits to the whole family are astounding.

Empowered mothers will teach their children to be good kids. She will teach her daughters and sons to believe in their capabilities. She will teach the values of peace, working hard, and spending time with your family.

Empowered mothers have more time for their husbands. Because -- let's be honest – when there's a new baby, dads take a backseat. But when mum is empowered, she is confident and peaceful. If Mummy's not stressed, Daddy's not going to be stressed.

Another important thing to consider is the role a husband or partner plays in empowering the mother. For a mother to be truly empowered, she must have support. She must have a spouse or partner that is on board with her, who is on her side, and who wants to help her with every part of being a parent.

It has been statistically shown that women typically perform most of the household duties. Consider the following chart, from a June, 2012 article on www.theatlantic.com:

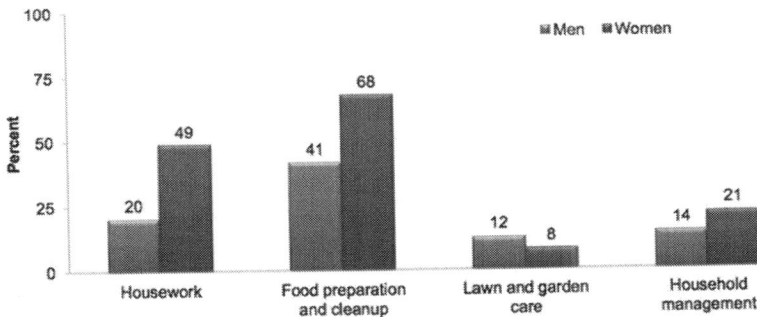

Percent of population who did household activities on an average day

It is also interesting to note that women in Europe especially seem to perform more household duties. Consider these statistics, from a July 2013 article from *The Huffington Post*:

- In the UK, 70 percent of all housework is done by women (and nearly two-thirds is done by women who work more than 30 hours a week).

- Nordic countries have the most equal distribution of domestic work, with Swedish women who work more than 30 hours per week doing less than two-thirds of the housework.

- Southern European countries lag behind, with the least equal distribution of housework.

- In Greece, over 80 percent of housework is done by women, and over three-quarters is done by women who work more than 30 hours per week

The same pattern holds true for American women. Consider the following statistics adapted from a 2013 report from the U.S. Bureau of Labor and Statistics:

- On an average day, 82 percent of women and 65 percent of men spent some time doing household activities.

- On the days they did household activities, women spent an average of 2.6 hours on such activities, while men spent 2.0 hours.

- On an average day, 20 percent of men did housework compared with 48 percent of women.

When working mothers have the added responsibility of performing most of the household work, it can create demands on her time that sometimes feel impossible and unrealistic. Many men and women accept this division of labour as normal, either because of deep-seated biases or simply as a continuation of the way they were raised.

Dividing household duties more evenly between spouses is vital not only to a mother's health and well-being, but also to the household in general. Fathers who are more involved in day-to-day management not only spend more time with their children, but also are more involved and engaged with their families.

In combination with helping with the everyday management of a household, having a supportive partner goes far beyond changing nappies and making bottles. It is about being invested in the mother and the children. It is about taking on responsibilities and admitting when they, too might need a little help.

Consider this story from a male colleague of mine:

You never really think about how much your interaction with your own parents affects your parenting choices. I only had two interactions with my dad, real ones, and I never really got to know him. I love my two children. I interact with them as much as possible. But when I have problems with them, I still question myself sometimes about the best way to discipline them, without resorting to spanking. It's a real struggle for me.

One day, when my little girl was four – she is now 14 – she got me upset, I kind of grabbed her – I didn't hit her, but I was definitely frustrated. My wife saw me and I'll never forget what she said - "If you ever do that again, you'll never see them again." I knew she meant it because she's German. She doesn't mess about.

I didn't hurt my daughter – but that was enough for me to evaluate myself, and decide that I wanted to change.

I knew there had to be some way, or some course out there I could learn to walk with children, raise my children, love them, but still discipline them effectively. But the only thing I could find was a fostering course — where they teach you to take care of foster children — you're basically raising someone else's child. It was all about bringing them into a positive environment.

I thought it might help, so I paid for this course, hoping to learn how to raise a child without smacking them, without being too much of a disciplinarian. It was such a wake-up call for me. I realized I didn't know much about kids and how to do certain things with them. It took me six months to pass this stupid course. I was frustrated and felt like I was completely incapable of parenting.

But I enjoyed it, and in the end, and it taught me a lot about parenting with both effectiveness and kindness.

This man saw a need in his family — for him to be a better parent. In turn, it helped his whole family. He found a solution and fixed it. This is a vital part of being an engaged partner.

Three of my babies are girls. I realize that one day, they're going to have their own lives. Somebody's son is going to marry one of my girls. They're going to have jobs and responsibilities and their own kids. I'm not going to be able to control what kind of marriage they have or what kind of work they do.

So I wonder, what can I do *now*? What can I do when they're little to make their life as joyful as possible in the future? This is what I can do: I can start now and empower the mothers of my generation - to teach their kids the right things, to be confident, to treat each other well. Then, when my girls are older, *their* husbands and colleagues and friends will hopefully treat my daughters the way they deserve to be treated.

This is my goal - I want to empower mums. If you can empower a mum and say, look, you can do this, and just give them the tools they need to be able to do it, you'll make the world a much better place.

Women are role models. They always have been and they always will be. They are role models for each other and they are role models for their children.

When I was growing up I thought I had the strictest mum on the planet. One time we actually took our mum to the church to report her to the Pastor, because she was so strict. She laughed at it and said how ridiculous this was.

And I remember thinking, "I will never be like her. When I have my kids, I'm going to let my kids go out, and I'm going to let my kids do all the things she's saying I can't do."

Well here I am a mother of four, and every single time I come up against a challenge or my sons ask me for this or that, well what do I do? I think back and ask myself, "What did my mother do?" I'm so thankful to her because I am the way I am, now, because of what she did then. And I was a very wild child, so if she hadn't done what she did for me, then I wouldn't be here.

Our kids are looking for role models. The model my mum set for me was one of hard work, following the rules, and doing what is right. But what's important to remember is that mums are more than just how they raise their kids – and it's equally important for your kids to see you as something *more* than a mother. Your daughters need to see that women can be successful, have hobbies, and make a difference in the world. Your sons need to see that it's okay for women to be strong, to make money, to do big things.

But if all your kid thinks you are is the person who cooks food, makes the beds, and cleans the house, well that's boring. They may think, "I don't want to be like that." But if your kids see you doing big things like, "Oh! My mum also hosts events," or "My mum also designs clothes," that's interesting.

Your kids are going to do what they're going to do with their lives. But if they see their mum's an inventor or an entrepreneur or a writer, or whatever, they want to be just like their mum. Not just because she told me to go to bed at 7pm and told me to stop watching my favourite program, but because she is an amazing human being.

I sing and speak on stage, but after I had kids, I stopped performing. Just a few months ago I decided to start doing it again and my kids came to watch me perform. When my kids are in the audience when I'm singing, the looks on their faces – well, I think I should record it and keep it for myself. They look at me like, "Wow. My mum can do that? You can do that?"

There is room in today's society for mothers to be *more* – whatever that means to each individual. If it means throwing yourself into motherhood, great. If it means writing a book or a screenplay, great. If it means working full time, great. Whatever it is, find time to do it. It doesn't have to be something huge, but something that your kids can say, "Oh, I like that my mum can do this. I can do what I want too, as well as doing the things that I have to."

It should also be clear with mothers that whether you're consciously making efforts to be a role model to your kids or not – *you are*. If they see you making poor choices or being lazy or all around unhappy, they will pick up on that and either resent you for it or follow in your footsteps.

Your children should be your motivation and incentive to be more and do more. Being their role model empowers you to get up in the morning. It makes you a better person.

One of the areas in which I see this having a huge impact is in how we, as women and mothers, talk about our appearances and our constant need to change and "improve" the way we look. I'm African – we don't typically have long hair. Many young African women feel the need to change who they are, in order to have long flowing hair or a lighter complexion. They think, *if I don't have my hair long and resilient, if my skin is not lighter, if my nails are not done a certain way, I'm not beautiful.*

As a result, many women in my culture wear wigs or extensions. Many are even buying them for their daughters. There is a child in my church who is ten years old and one day I saw her wearing a wig. I couldn't understand why this young girl was wearing wig. But then I realized that her mum was always wearing wigs.

I'm not saying that there is something wrong with wearing a wig or enhancing your appearance. But kids today have constant exposure to the internet, social media, television, and other media that tells them they have to look or act a certain way. If you take your 10-year-old child to the salon and get them a wig, you're telling the child that she's not pretty enough with her own hair. She is always going to need a wig to feel that she is pretty enough.

The first people children try to model themselves after are their parents. In fact, my younger cousins used to ask me to take them to her school's parents evening, because they didn't want their parents to go. They would say, "Please Winnie, can you come and bring your Burberry bag?" Kids want to show their friends that their parents are it!

I have a colleague, who is of African descent and his wife is German. Their daughter is obsessed with having straight hair, because her mum has straight hair. She just can't understand why her mother has hair that is always straight and why her own hair always curls up. He tells her it's because she's a mixed child, and she's getting it, but she still insists she wants her hair straight. She wants to be like the person she is around the most.

So if we, as mums, are obsessed with the way we look, we are telling our kids that in order to be beautiful you have to drastically change yourself. So as parents, don't wait for somebody else to be the role model. I really believe that as mums, we need to show our children what it means to be confident. We need to show them what a real person looks like.

If, as a mother, you raise your child up to say, actually, having your own natural hair is beautiful, and you praise them, and you affirm them, say things like, "Wow, what beautiful hair you have!" Then take pictures and put them up on the wall in your house, you're showing the child, it's okay, you're beautiful.

The best way to do this is to go back to your roots and enhance what you have. So work with what you have and show your kids it's ok to have your natural hair and find ways to make that natural hair fantastic. Look after yourself. Look after your hair. Be sure you show your kids that this is what natural beauty looks like. Your kids will emulate you and want to be like that.

Another thing I hear women complaining about is their weight. This is a way in which mothers can show their children the benefits of making healthy, responsible decisions, and working hard to make positive changes in their lives.

Mothers affect their children's behaviour in a million ways, not just in the way they think about their looks. We, as mums, can set good examples about healthy eating, making responsible decisions, and so much more.

When I was growing up, if I wanted to go out – forget it. I wasn't allowed to stay out after 10 pm. If we were out, we were out with our parents. And that lasted until I was about 20 years old. Even now, as an adult, I have my own keys, I have my own house, I have my own everything, but when I'm out at night and it's after 10:00pm, something inside me says, *I shouldn't really be here.* Like I really think if I'm going to stay out after 10pm, it's got to be a really good reason why I'm out after 10pm. Where did I get this from? From when my mother showed me that you shouldn't do this.

But now, in some neighbourhoods, you go out and you find 4 year old kids out at 8pm, riding their bicycles. I think that's insane. What are they doing out at 8pm, riding a bicycle? How is that child going to concentrate in class? They're not going to do it.

I believe that mothers are the most powerful force on the planet. If we're not being role models for our children, somebody else will. This may sound strong, but I really feel that if mothers were more involved, and being good role models, many children out there who are currently making poor choices wouldn't be doing the things they're doing. Empowered, confident mothers can change the world.

Research says that between the ages of 0-7, kids are embedded with everything they're ever going to learn. After that, they try to exercise some autonomy and start making their own decisions. But what we teach them when they're young sticks with them.

Another colleague told me that his mother told him that she could smell him 100 miles away if he was smoking cigarettes. When he left home for the first time, there was no way in a million years you could ever convince him to light a cigarette or date a girl who smoked. It was a test for him. If there was a girl he liked and he saw her smoking, straight away, all he could think is that his mother could smell him 100 miles away. Even though it was totally illogical that she would actually be able to smell him, it was so embedded in his head that he wouldn't even date a smoker.

That's incredible. That's the power a mother has. And if we stop being depressed and feeling guilty and stop listening to the media telling us we're not good enough, we'll realize we are. We can make a difference now and in generations to come and all the rest of it. We need to start now. Get off your sofa, stop feeling sorry for yourself, stop being depressed, stop feeling guilty, and get up.

I believe that sometimes we get lost in all the things we think we're supposed to be doing. We know we need to feed and clothe our children, teach them to read, sign them up for activities, expose them to culture, etc., etc. And all of those things are important. But what is more important is that we make time to do the small things that have a big impact.

Below is a list of small things I try to do every day that helps my children to build confidence. Hopefully they will remember these moments, rather than the times I lost my temper or was stressed out.

- Tell your kids you love them. Every day. Make sure they know that you love them even when you're angry with them.

- Tell them stories about when they were a baby.

- Tell them about things you've struggled with in your life and how you overcame it.

- Leave notes in their lunchbox.

- Give them an important responsibility and trust that they can do it.

- Listen to them and ask questions in response.

- Ask what they're thinking about or what they think of a certain topic or issue.

Chapter 3

Take a Breath – Empower Yourself

One of the things I realized when I had my first baby is that something happens to a woman when she gives birth. Motherly instincts kick in. I'd never had it before – I didn't even know it was a thing. But I was so in tune with my child, it was unbelievable. I wasn't a medical expert, but if something was wrong with my baby, I knew it.

I believe that every mother has this instinct, but it gets buried by all the noise she hears from family, friends, the internet, and television. All these things tell her how everything *should* go, instead of just addressing the way it *is* going. Then she loses confidence in what she knows to be right. As fantastic as information is, one of the things that information has done to mothers is that it has taken away that motherly instinct to the point that women no longer want to think. They just want somebody to tell them what to do.

Sometimes when I meet a client, they say to me, "Oh, Winnie, I don't know what to do with this baby. I don't know." The rest of our conversation goes like this:

Winnie: "Who spends the longest amount of time with your baby?"

Mother: "I do."

Winnie: "Okay. I'm Winnie, I'm the expert, I've come in, but I'm only going to spend a few hours with your baby, and half the time, your baby's going to be sleeping. So who's going to be the expert as far as your baby's concerned?"

Mother: "Well, me."

Winnie: "Exactly."

Mothers forget that they spend more time with their baby than anyone else. You observe your child, and, along with a few guidelines, you figure out what your baby likes and needs. You'll know if your baby loves swaddling or not. You'll figure out if your baby needs to be burped once or twice during a feeding. It's cause and effect; when I did this, this happened. When I did that, that happened. So if I do this, and they cry, maybe they don't want this. If I do that and they stop crying or fall right asleep, then they probably liked it.

Simply observing their baby will allow mothers to have the confidence that they can figure it out. The result may not be "accurate" as far as the medical community is concerned, but it works for you and for your baby.

A great example of this is formula feeding. There are hundreds of brands and variety of formula. Does your baby need soy? Gentle formula? Formula with low iron? Formula with probiotics? There are so many options that often, unless there is some known medical condition, it's okay to just randomly pick one to try. So let's say you try a regular formula with DHA. Baby seems fussy, gassy, and often rejects the bottle. So you switch to a gentle formula and suddenly baby is happy, eating a full bottle, and falling peacefully asleep after every feeding.

Which do you stick with? The gentle formula, of course. But you didn't need a doctor to tell you that. You are capable of figuring it out. And once you give yourself permission to be the expert on your baby, you will move forward with confidence in every decision you make.

This confidence will allow mothers to stand up for their baby's needs. Unfortunately, many "experts" seem to think every mother's losing it or that there is some kind of medical explanation for any issue she may be having with baby. So before such people come in and tell a mother that there's something wrong with her or her baby, she needs to be in a place where she has the confidence to say, "Actually, I know that's what you're saying, but that's not what my baby does. I know you're saying *this*, but actually, no, that's not correct. *This* is what works for my baby."

If they ask why, she can say, "Because when my baby does this, he's happy. He's smiling, he's not crying, and he's pooing and peeing as normal. My baby's fine." But she can only say that if she has that confidence.

There is a place for people like me to come in and help, but before we even come in, mothers need to have that confidence as a mum. *She* knows her baby. *She* is the expert. I'm just here to encourage them.

There are great nannies out there, but every baby needs a mum. I don't believe mums lose confidence because they don't *want* to mother – it's because they think they can't do it, so they give up and bring in people to do it for them.

I want to encourage more mums to occupy their position and do it confidently and gladly rather than just giving up.

Here are some more of my favourite tips for empowering yourself as a mum.

Fake it 'til you make it. Babies don't come with a manual. We aren't born knowing how to heat up a bottle or change a nappy. But we love our babies. You want to do what's best for them. Let that guide you. If you feel like sometimes you're barely holding it together, that's ok. You'll learn. Pretend like you know what you're doing and eventually you'll be able to do it with your eyes closed.

Get over guilt. Whether it's about returning to work, not spending enough time with all of your children, or because you forgot to wish your husband a happy anniversary, we will all make mistakes. Get over it. No one is a perfect mother. Trying to be will only cause you more stress. Let your children see you make mistakes and also see how you did your best to successfully resolve the situation and learn from it.

I believe that guilt is the single biggest thing standing in the way of every mother becoming an empowered mum. We're going to talk more about that in the next chapter.

Don't compete. Don't worry about the woman you know with triplets who are always clean, with perfect hair, and a spotless house. We're all good at something – focus on what you know you do well and draw confidence from the fact that your children are healthy and taken care of.

Lower your standards. You don't have to have an immaculate house or the perfect outfit. Do what you can, when you can. Focus on what is most important to you and you'll feel better when you're doing your favourite things well.

Have fun. Kids are fun! Laugh, play, and smile, and don't worry about whether their apple sauce is organic or their toys are educational. Your children will remember your silly songs and games - they will remember the *time* they spent with you.

Sometimes we get lost in the drudgery and day-to-day stress of having a young family. It's easy for the fun to get lost. Kids can make us feel young again, can help us find the wonder and innocence in the world.

Below I've listed some of my favourite activities that force me to slow down and appreciate the wonder and delight that are my children.

- Have a dance party.

- Tell a silly story, and everyone contributes!

- Go on a nature walk.

- Play a rhyming game.

- Ask your kids to tell you about their dreams.

- Lay in the grass and look for shapes in the clouds.

- Talk about what they want to be when they grow up.

- Show them pictures of you when you were little.

The best way I illustrate the power of empowerment is to tell a story. Not long ago, I was working with a family. The mum, let's call her Susan, had a three-year-old boy and she had just had her second baby. Susan was so stressed out. She was having trouble functioning, doubting her abilities as a mother, and was just an all-around mess. I knew I had to get to the bottom of it because her depression was reaching concerning levels.

After speaking with her and other medical professionals that had worked with her, it seemed as though the stress boiled down to this: she could not figure out how to fit enough love in for this new baby. When she had her first son, she spent all her time with him. She loved him. They did everything for him, and now, here comes baby number two, and now she's thinking, *How do I give the same love, the same attention to baby number two that I gave to baby number one and not make baby number one feel left out?*

She couldn't do it. She just could not figure it out, and she became so stressed to the point that she developed severe post-natal depression, almost psychosis, where she was having thoughts of killing the baby.

When I was given the job, the agency warned me in advance that this mum was really ill. I was told to watch out for the baby, that she had tried to kill the baby. They told me that they had sent in a few nannies and they'd all failed and left. So I was going into the situation with the assumption that it was a lost cause and I wouldn't succeed. But I love challenges, so in I went.

When I began the job, I had all of this information playing in my mind; this woman's mad, this woman's crazy. So every time she would come near the baby, I would find myself thinking; *Stay away from the baby, stay away from the baby*. After a while, I caught myself. After all, this is a mum. If every time she comes near her own child I'm making her feel like she's crazy, then she's going to behave exactly like a crazy person.

So I decided I wasn't going to assume she wanted to hurt her baby. Yes, I'd make sure the baby was safe, but I was not going to take away this woman's power as a mother.

I racked my brain for what I could do to give her some of her power back and began thinking about what it's like to be a new mum. It's always about the baby – when people buy a new mum a gift, it's really a gift for the baby. It's very rare that somebody buys a gift for the mum. No one's ever bought me a present as a mum and said, "Oh, congratulations for having a wonderful baby!" Mums get socks, baby bottles, baby clothes. Nobody ever buys me anything. But hold on, I've just carried this baby for nine months. Surely, I deserve something!

So the next time I was on my way to Susan's house, I stopped at a department store and bought a really pretty notepad and wrapped it up nicely. The baby was sleeping when I got there, so I went to Susan and said to her, "I bought you something." You should have seen the look on her face.

"You've bought me something? Oh, my God, and you're just like a nanny, and you bought me something?"

I said, "Yeah, I bought you something. Open it."

We sat down and when she opened it she said, "Oh, my God, this is so pretty, but, Winnie, what am I going to do with a notebook?"

I said, "Remember you said to me you can't sleep because you have all these things going through your head? The next time you can't sleep, get that little pretty book and write down the stuff that's going through your head, just write it down. I found when you write stuff down, you stop thinking about it because, okay, I've written it down, I'm going to deal with that next time."

She said, "Actually, that makes a lot of sense. Yeah, I'm going to do that."

So she began to trust me. She realized that I wasn't looking at her like she was crazy. I was looking at her like she was a human, like a mum. So we started talking.

I said, "So what is it that you're finding difficult?"

She responded, "Winnie, you're so lucky you're a mother of three, and how do you do it?"

I said, "How do I do what?"

"How are you able to love all your kids the same?"

"Well, why do you ask?"

"Because the reason why I'm struggling so much, because I don't know how to love the baby."

That sounds like an awful thing to say – and she felt awful for feeling that way! But here is the rest of the story: Her first child was incredibly clingy. Every time she would hold the baby, her oldest would say, "No, Mummy, that's mean," because he still thought of that as his space – why is this baby coming in and taking over? He wasn't going to have it.

And Susan, because she wasn't sure how to handle it and was so used to addressing the needs of her older child, would, without even thinking about it, walk away from the baby and just forget.

For example, one day the baby was in the bath and the older child walked in – don't forget the baby is in the bath with water in the bath – and she unconsciously goes to help her older son. Guess what happened to the baby? The baby began to drown in the bath. Luckily, the nanny ran in, but all she saw was the baby alone in the water. Her assumption was that the baby was dying and the mum had done it on purpose. Susan was accused of trying to kill her child.

That wasn't the case at all. She was lonely, confused, suffering from depression and she just didn't know how to love both her babies at the same time.

Once I realized what was really happening, I suggested that she take time out every day – even if it was for only 20 minutes – when her older son wasn't home, and forgetting about everybody else. Just spending time alone with her baby. Holding him, looking at him, just taking him in to see what happened.

After that first day, she told me, "Oh, my God, this is so fantastic." I said, "Once you've mastered 20 minutes, try 30 minutes, and then when your older son's around, do it together so that he comes to realize, 'okay, this little man is not stealing my attention, but actually, I'm helping Mummy to look after him,', so that your older child becomes involved in the attention that you give to the baby."

I worked with this family for a long time. The agency asked me, "How in the world did you do it?" All I did was empower this woman. I told her, "Look, you're not crazy. Things are a bit hard. It's challenging to raise two kids, but this is how you do it." Once she realized that there wasn't anything wrong with her and that she did have the ability to love and care for her children, she regained confidence in herself.

In fact, she fell pregnant again. When the agency found out, they were like, "Oh, my God! Oh, no! She's pregnant again!" But actually, this time around, she's done so much better because she took the lessons she learned from last time and now she says, "I can do this."

We will all have moments as parents when we question our capabilities, when we feel like we make the wrong decisions for our children, or when we feel just plain exhausted and worn out by everything that needs to be done.

In those moments, we don't always have a chance to talk it out or ask for help. That's why I've provided the following list of inspirational quotes. You can write these down, keep them in your phone, or memorize them. Whatever it takes, just have them handy so that when you start questioning yourself you can be reminded that you are an amazing mum – and your kids are lucky to have you.

"A woman is like a tea bag: you cannot tell how strong she is until you put her in hot water." – Nancy Reagan

"Figure out who you are separate from your family, and the man or woman you're in a relationship with. Find who you are in this world and what you need to feel good alone. I think that's the most important thing in life. Find a sense of self because with that, you can do anything else." – Angelina Jolie

"There is no way to be a perfect mother, and a million ways to be a good one." - Jill Churchill

"Women do not have to sacrifice personhood if they are mothers. They do not have to sacrifice motherhood in order to be persons. Liberation was meant to expand women's opportunities, not to limit them. The self-esteem that has been found in new pursuits can also be found in mothering." - Elaine Heffner

"A mother's arms are more comforting than anyone else's." - Diana, Princess of Wales

"Though motherhood is the most important of all the professions requiring more knowledge than any other department in human affairs there was no attention given to preparation for this office." - Elizabeth Cady Stanton

"A baby will make love stronger, days shorter, nights longer, bankroll smaller, home happier, clothes shabbier, the past forgotten, and the future worth living for." —Pablo Picasso

"There will be so many times you feel like you've failed, but in the eyes, *heart and mind of your child you are super mum."* – Stephanie Precourt

"Being a mother is learning about strengths you didn't know you had... and dealing with fears you didn't know existed." - Linda Wooten

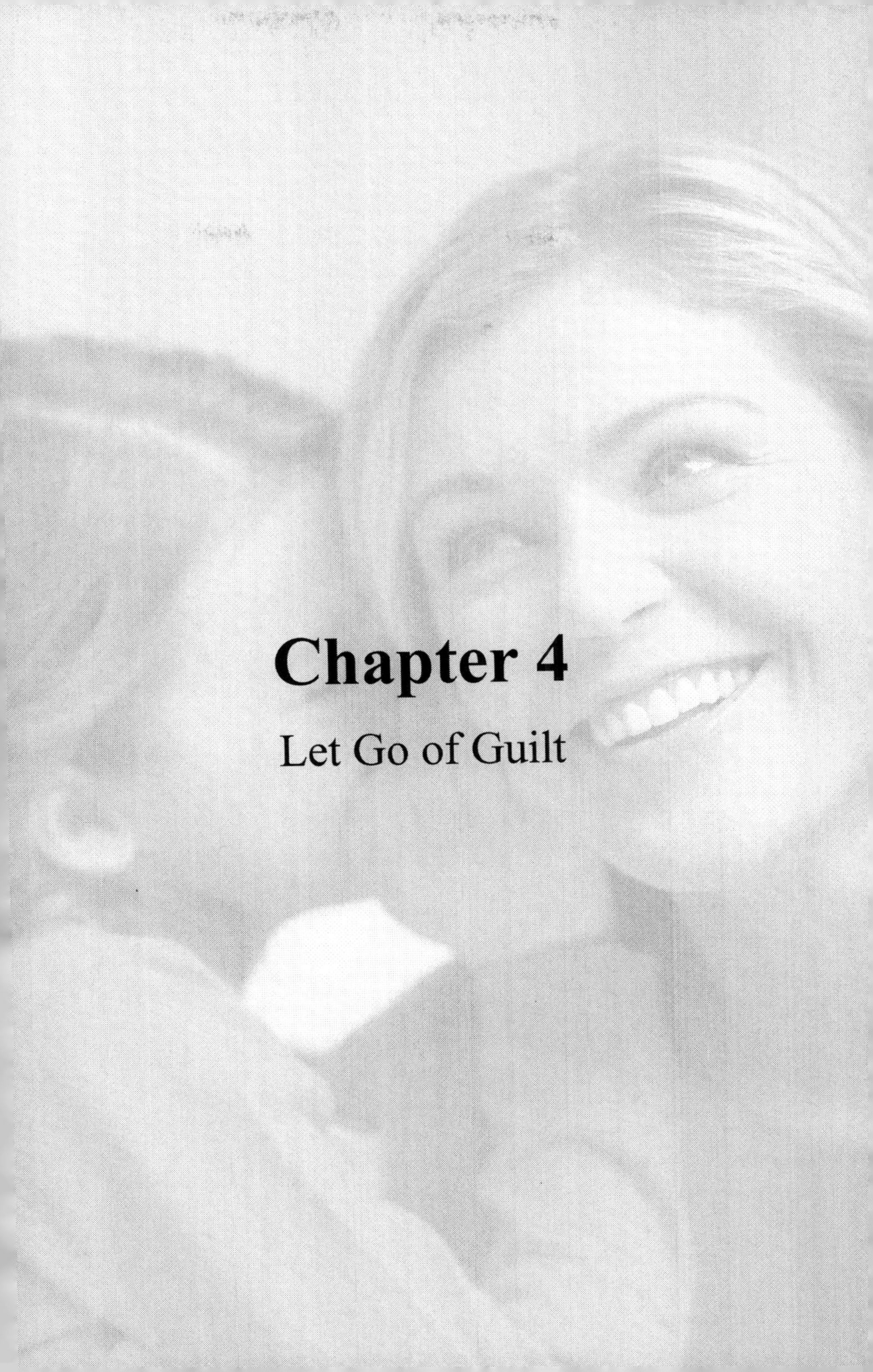

Chapter 4

Let Go of Guilt

Every mother has it, whether you work outside of the home or stay at home with your kids. Whether you have money or you're poor. Whether you have help or you're doing it all alone. At some point, every mother has felt guilty. Most of the time we feel guilty for things we can't control or things that, in the end, don't really matter.

I believe that the only way to break out of this cycle of guilt is to provide mothers with the tools, resources, and advice they need that will allow them to be successful both at home and at work. Most women believe that they can't do both – that for them to be a good mum, their work has to suffer. Or to be a good employee they can't focus on their kids.

I *know* that we can do both. The problem is convincing ourselves that we deserve to have success both at work and home and learning the skills necessary to do that.

Find Yourself

I think the first step is taking the time to find yourself outside of work and home. The person you were before you had kids is still there – but you've probably changed your priorities so drastically that you can't remember. But that part of you doesn't disappear when you have a baby, it just becomes the lowest priority. I think it's important that we make an effort to bring those things that made us happy before we had kids back into our lives.

So many times I meet women and I ask them, why don't you go out with your friends? Inevitably they say, "Oh, I can't do that." When I ask them why they say they feel guilty. They don't feel they can still go out and have a good time and still be mothers. And when they do, they feel guilty because they don't think it's acceptable and sometimes they feel that other women would look down on them and judge them for being out and away from their children.

But that's just not true. If you don't do that and you're looking out for your kids every single day, seven days a week, getting up in the morning, you dress the children, you bathe them, you cook the food for your husband, where's the stuff for you?

It's not just about what you're *supposed* to do, but also about the fact that you're still a woman. You're a wife and mother, but the woman in you still exists. You have ambitions; you have things you want to do. You have a bucket list of things you want to do before you check out.

If we tell women that all they're allowed to be is a mum, we are putting them in a box. And quite frankly, I am sick and tired of people putting mothers in a box and saying because you're a mother, you can't work. Or you can't go out and spend time with your friends.

Says who? I can work, given the right tools, given the right people in place to help me do so, I can still be effective. And I think if mothers were given the support and encouragement to do both, the world would be a much better place for it.

After all, we think nothing of it when men go to work and have their hobbies on the weekends. *Mums can too.*

Before I started as a night nanny, I felt guilty all the time. Like if I went to work and then also left the kids with my husband or my mum, I felt terrible because I felt like I was letting somebody else do my job for me. But what I eventually realized was no, I just needed a time out.

And you know what happened when I went out? I came back feeling fantastic. Not only did I feel refreshed and a little bit more like my "old" self, but I missed my kids and was ready to devote more time and attention to them. It's like I came out of a box and was able to see things from a different perspective. It's a *good thing* for you to be able to go out and do what you enjoy and then come back.

As a maternity nurse, I know I'm doing a good job if a client says to me, "Winnie, I'm going out for a meal with my friends." It means what I'm doing is worth it – she feels confident enough to know her child is really taken care of and she can now go and have a night out. Every time that happens when I'm doing a job, I know I'm ready to leave because I know this woman feels confident enough that she can actually go out and leave her baby who's 6 or 8 weeks old.

Taking care of yourself is good for you, your children, and your marriage.

I see a lot of guilt with really successful women. I worked with one woman who was incredibly successful; she was an editor at a magazine and also a mother of four. She said something particularly interesting to me. She was in Europe somewhere, sitting in a room with all of these powerful women doing fantastic things and she says all of them couldn't help feeling guilty. They were all successful in their fields, leading fulfilling lives, providing for their families, and *still* they felt guilty.

In all areas of our lives we have certain expectations of ourselves and also, those expectations others have of us. It's difficult to know how to prioritize. When working mums have a baby they may pick up on the fact that their male bosses may be thinking "Oh great. Now she's not going to be able to do her job." So working mums feel like they have to show their bosses and colleagues they can still do their job the same way they did before. But you can't.

Conversely, when a woman has a baby, society and maybe even her family tells her that she should enjoy every second, breastfeed exclusively, feed the baby only homemade organic food, and have proper stimulation for baby every second of every day. So working mums feel like they have to work and be supermum. But you can't.

No mother ever has to feel this way. I say yes, they should raise their kids, but there should be a balance. Most of the time when women get it wrong and give working mums a bad name is when they go all out: "Yeah, I'm going to go for my career and let the money raise the kid." If your job takes you away 24 hours a day, if your job means you are away most of the day, then your priorities have to change. There are ways to address this to make sure you get quality time in with your kids and do your job. You have to strike a balance.

Parents feel guilty when they don't know how to strike that balance. Women don't think they're allowed to have it both ways and the world tells us we can't have it both ways. Our husbands tell us we're not allowed to have it both ways. Our boss at work tells us we're not allowed to have it both ways.

This is why empowered women – women who don't live with this guilt – have the right people in place to help them do the things that they used to do before, so that they are still be able to raise their own children.

There is a way to overcome this guilt. Firstly, find out why you feel guilty. Most women will tell me, "Actually, I don't know why I'm feeling guilty, I just feel guilty." I worked with one mum who had two kids at home, and her youngest was 6 or 8 weeks old. She wasn't getting enough sleep, so I came in to help. She works in marketing and one of the first things she says to me is, "I don't think I can do this. I don't think I can give up my job and do this whole mother thing. I've got somebody sucking on my breasts all day long and I could be out there with my friends, going out to lunch but I can't because I've got this baby here, doing this all day long and I just feel completely powerless that I just have to give in and just do that. What can I do?"

She was feeling depressed because she felt she could no longer go out and have meals with her friends or even just have a chat with her friends because now she had to be there feeding the baby and playing with the baby and all the rest of it. She was feeling guilty because she didn't feel like she wanted to be with her kids every second of every day – and she didn't want to give up her career. She felt like it was either one or the other.

She was a woman who was used to having lunches, having her own time. So I told her we were going to find a way for her to do some of the things she used to do before but also make sure that her kids were taken care of. Her priorities simply had to change. Her child was now priority number one, but her own needs didn't have to be so far down the list. All she had to do was be sure that her baby's needs were met and that they wouldn't be compromised.

I told her to look at her schedule and find a small window of time where she could do something she enjoyed. She said Mondays were good. So I said "Ok, right now, your baby needs to eat, he needs to sleep, he needs to have his nappy changed. So on Mondays, when the baby is sleeping during the day, call that your time. Call a friend and ask her to lunch during those two hours. You arrange for someone to come over right before you leave. You can feed the baby, then the baby takes a nap. You'll know, wherever you are, your baby is sleeping, so even if you were at home, there's nothing you'd be doing with the baby at that particular time.

It was like a light bulb came on in her brain. She came back and, because she got to experience what she used to have before, she was excited and so happy.

And guess what her husband said? "Winnie, you've given me my wife back." Before they got married, that's the woman he saw and that he fell in love with. Now, all he sees is this woman who is depressed and complaining about kids and in the meantime he doesn't want to come home early because he's just going to hear, "You've been at work all day, you don't understand what I have to go through and then you complain." But giving her some time to herself allowed him to get that woman back that he fell in love with.

You don't have to feel guilty. You can have a system, you can have a routine, whatever you want to call it -- that allows you to make sure that your baby's priorities are met and you can still go out and have a good time. It takes a bit of practice because at first you feel a bit guilty, but afterwards you realize it's not affected your child at all.

I'm not saying it's going to be easy. If you want to have some kind of your life back, you need to understand that you're going to need to have certain things in place to be able to have that. You may need to work a little bit harder, on a schedule, on asking for help, and rearranging your priorities.

Letting go of guilt has to be a conscious decision on your part. You need to tell yourself that you are going to do the things you need to do to take care of yourself and your family. The rest of this chapter details some of my favourite tips and tricks for gaining more control and perspective in your life.

Have a Schedule

One of the most important things to help you prioritize is having a schedule. You must have some kind of a schedule. My motto is that I don't wait for the time, I make the time. I keep a detailed schedule for all of my kids' activities, and mine and my husband's. I put time in there for the things I need, in addition to everything my family needs. There's never going to be a day as a mum, when you think, "Oh, I've got nothing to do today!" It's never gonna happen!

From the day you have the child, that's it. Boom! Many times before you have kids, you think *Oh, what am I going to do today?* Forget that. You have to make the time. And how are you going to make the time? Put it on paper. Sometimes you're running around like a headless chicken, where at the end of the day you're not even sure what you did all day. How often do you find yourself running around doing things that aren't actually helping you, and they're not actually helping your husband or your kids? Many of us think that we should be busy because we're mums; that we're just supposed to be busy.

But putting it down on paper means getting it out of your head, prioritizing your to-do list, and then you can see exactly where you're spending your time and where you have time to make for yourself and your husband.

Use a family calendar like the sample below from calendarsquick.com to organize your whole family:

Weekly Family Calendar
Week of January 3, 2010

	Sunday 3	Monday 4	Tuesday 5	Wednesday 6	Thursday 7	Friday 8	Saturday 9
Laurie							
Sam							
Michael							
Brian							
Abbie							

http://www.calendarsquick.com

Be Prepared to Let Go

One thing I think we can all agree on at this point is that sometimes mums just need a break. But it's sometimes difficult to do that without feeling guilty or nervous. We worry that if we leave our children with a babysitter they will get hurt or will be exposed to something that we didn't want them exposed to. The best way to be able to let go is to feel comfortable with the person you leave your children with.

So one of the rules in my house is that my kids aren't allowed to go to anybody's house unless I know who that person is, or at least have a good idea. When I know where I'm sending my children, I can take that time off and actually relax.

Just the other day, I kind of made a mistake. I have a new neighbour who has just moved in next door. She's a teacher with two kids and we were both coming up the stairs at the same time. She asked us if we wanted to go to the park. I declined, because we had just got home and I didn't want to go out again. But my son really wanted to go, so she offered to take him. I agreed.

And as soon as they went around the corner, I realized, *I have no idea who this person is.* I didn't have her phone number, she didn't have mine, and I didn't have any way of getting in touch with her. All the mistakes I could make, I made them. So I was worrying the whole time, wondering when they would be back. She'd said they'd be gone about one hour, but what if it was a few hours? What if I needed to leave? What if there was an emergency? I was a mess.

Luckily they came back after two hours. And she said the same thing I had been thinking the whole time, "I just realized I don't have your number, and you don't have my number!" I would have saved myself a lot of trouble if I had been prepared or asked some questions.

It worked out in the end and she actually told me something about my son that leads to another survival tip that I live by as a mum.

Make Safety Rules

It's no secret to anyone with children that most kids seem hell-bent on giving us all grey hair. They jump off furniture, dash into the street, run too fast, the list goes on and on. Trying to keep young children safe could be a full time job. This only adds to a mum's stress levels.

I combat this by having clear rules in my house and when we're out and about. Most importantly, I enforce them. So I know that if I have my hands full at the market, I can let go of my daughter's hand to grab my wallet, and I know she won't run away. I can run to the bathroom at home because my children know not to go into the kitchen when I'm not there.

Of course there will always be accidents and emergencies that we can't foresee. But having ground rules that are enforced helps alleviate some of the stress of keeping our children safe.

When my new neighbour brought my son home, she said to me, "Your son is incredible." When I asked her why, she told me that when she told him and her children to run off and play and her children tried to run a little too far away, my son had said, "We can't go there because your mum can't see us!"

One of the things I teach my kids is that if we're out, mummy has to be able to see you. So when my neighbour told me this story, I thought, *thank God, I've taught him something!*

This showed me that even though he went off, now I don't have to feel guilty or worried. I can be confident that as a mum, even though I'm not there, my son is going to be as safe as possible. If only I had asked for her phone number, I would have really been able to enjoy the afternoon!

Time management

You must be organized. There's no two ways around it. If you're going to work and raise a family you must be organized. You need to make sure your kids have eaten, and if they're going to school, their uniforms are done, they've done their homework. If you don't have some kind of a system that sets forth when you do homework, when you do bedtime stories, at such a time you make sure their uniforms are clean, at such a time you make sure they're prepared for the following day. If you don't do that, it's never going to happen.

I always say to mums – and I say it to myself – if you want anything to happen, you can't sit around waiting for that time to come, you have to make the time. So for a working mother, you must be organized. You must learn how to manage your time, you must learn how to prioritize what's really important, and you must define where the priorities rank in terms of importance.

Your Personal Health

There's no way you're going to be able to look after your kids and go to work if you're not healthy. So that means you take care of you, eat the right food, make time to eat. Many times as mothers sometimes you don't find the time to eat, you're running up and down and you forget to find the time to eat. So making sure you look after yourself is number 1, in order to be able to look after everyone else. Make sure you plan for that, even if it means you add supplements and vitamins to your diet.

Surround Yourself with Support

Be mindful of who you listen to and who you hang around with. Try to find other mothers who are successful, working mothers or mothers who are content staying at home. If you're going to hang around with all of your friends who are single and don't have any kids and they're all saying, "Oh we're going to go out and do this, we're going to go out and spend this kind of money" for example, you're going to feel terrible all the time. They're not trying to make you feel bad on purpose, but they may look at you and think, *Oh, she never goes anywhere, what's the point of asking her?* So already you're putting yourself in a corner. But if you spend more time with other mothers in situations similar to yours, who are successful in what they're doing, you will be learning from them and they will also be learning from you.

Stand up for Yourself

This can be just as important for stay at home mums, but is particularly true for working mothers. Like I said before, when you have children, it doesn't mean you lose who you are. If you were a fantastic TV presenter before, you can still be that person and raise your children. So many times people don't know how to have it both ways – to be that fantastic TV presenter and be a mother at the same time.

Many years ago, we were living in a different world; most women found it more rewarding to stay at home than go out and work. But now things are very different. A large percentage – 54.3% around the world – of mothers work. Many women find working fulfilling and beneficial for their families.

But working mums do face many obstacles. Some bosses or employers are hesitant about working mothers. They think her kids are going to fall ill and she's going to take a few days off, and they have all these fears that as a parent you're not going to be able to give the same productivity as somebody else who's not a parent.

I disagree. I believe you can still be productive, but in order for you to do that, you have to take on board some principles and tools that are going to help you remain at the same level as the other employees.

For example, I read an article recently about a working mother who said that employers are scared that if her child falls ill, she is going to be at home and would take days off. And she says, yes, if my son falls ill, I may take days off, but we're living in an advanced technology era. I'll take my laptop home with me and when my son is ill, sleeping in bed, I could be at home doing my job. I'm still going to be as productive. I may not be physically in the office, but I'm going to be doing my job.

In the above example, the mother was able to work from home. If you are a mother whose job requires you to be present physically at work, the above may not be possible for you. However, I believe with the right network of trustworthy people, you will be able to take minimal time off (if that works for your family).

I also want to recognise that there are situations where a mother may need to take a lot of time off. For example, if the baby is diagnosed with a condition requiring both mother and the baby to be in hospital. In these cases I would put the baby first.

Traditionally, it has been, if you're working, you're in the office. But that's all changed now. When I was working as a personal assistant, I told my bosses that I could do my job at home and they were saying, "No no, no, you can't do your job at home." I said, "Let's try it for two weeks." I suggested this because the Olympics were in London and they really had no choice. Transportation was crazy and employers were being encouraged to let their employees work at home. And guess what? Everything worked fine doing my job at home.

I think traditionally employers think if you're not in the office you're not being productive. So I know we as mothers also actually believe that – like maybe I'm not going to be good enough. But we can prove to our employers and everyone else that we can do whatever we put our minds to.

Stand up for yourself, be assertive, and use the tools we've talked about to make your life just what you want it to be for both you and your family.

Chapter 5

Ask for Help

I have somebody that helps me take care of my kids. I'm a nanny, and I have someone that helps me take care of my kids. There is *nothing* wrong with asking for help.

Being a parent is hard – some mothers just need emotional help and support. Others need more tangible help, like picking kids up from school. We all need help.

The important thing to remember is that there is a difference between asking for help and letting someone else raise your kids. Kids need their mother. However imperfect or busy you think you are, your kids need you. Asking for help makes you a better parent – but the best parents devote what time they can to their kids.

I'm a big believer of this: if you want your child to be like the nanny, let the nanny raise them. I grew up with a mum who is also a fantastic woman. I'm so glad I was raised by a confident woman. She wasn't perfect – but she was the best mum she could be and I've taken all of those lessons with me into my adulthood.

My dad died when I was about seven and my mum took over. She came to the UK from Africa. She brought us all over to the UK and when she came here, her friends said to her,

"Oh, it's so sad that you're going to lose your kids." When she asked what they meant, they said, "Because," they said, "they're all going to go off, and they're going to become like many of the kids I have seen in this neighbourhood, never studying, never doing anything," and my mum always replied, "I said one thing, my kids will not be like the kids that you see walking on the streets around here, not doing anything."

My mum took a stand on the things that were most important to her. She had to ask for help, but she was there when it *mattered* – she instilled in us all the values she thought were most important.

Help for mothers can come in a variety of forms; help from your partner, help from your family and friends, professional help, and help from your "village." After all, didn't someone once say that it takes a village to raise a child? There is no shame in asking for help. Actually, it's *vital* that mothers ask for help. No one can do it alone.

Leave it to the Professionals

Nannies can become part of the family, and that's great. After all, you want someone taking care of your child who truly cares about their health and well-being.

What I Believe a Nanny's Responsibilities Are

I'm going to talk about my experiences as a night nanny, but much of this is applicable to day nannies also.

Night nannies usually work from 9:00 p.m. until 7:00 a.m. Generally, you're there to help the mum get some sleep at night. Babies will wake up almost every three hours at night and some every hour, hence mums don't get any sleep, so you're there to help the mum and take over when the baby wakes up.

Once the baby goes to sleep, you also go to sleep, and then you wake up when the baby wakes up. You take care of the baby by preparing the baby for mum to feed, for example, if the baby needs a nappy change. If the mum is bottle feeding, and there are bottle to be sterilized, you will do the sterilizing of the bottles. Most of the time, we don't administer medicine, but you're there, basically, if the mum needs you to help her to show her how to breastfeed, show the baby to latch onto the breast correctly, and so on. You're there to assist the mum.

For example, first-time mums who don't know much about having a baby or taking care of the baby, you're there to be the person they can turn around and say, "Okay. How do I do this?"

Many times, I'm just there to talk. I find out from the client what they are really looking for from this service. Some people will say, "Actually, I just want a good night's sleep," and in that case, I say, "Okay. No problem. Just show me where the baby things are, where the nappies are, where the clothes are for if the baby needs changing, where's the milk?" They will show you where everything is, and off they will go to sleep.

I keep a diary of everything that happens in the night. When the baby wakes up in the morning, I update the mum on what happened that night, and off I go.

There are lots of nanny agencies out there. What I try to do different is hire nannies who are able to empower women, nannies who are able to sit down and have a conversation with a woman and say, "Well, actually, it's okay. I've been there before," and be on her team. If given a chance, I will always hire a mother. You can teach someone how to be a nanny, but there are some things you can only learn as a mum. You're either a mum or you're not and I want our services to be different in the sense that the mum is confident that you know what you're talking about, apart from being there to wash a bottle, or being able to teach a baby how to latch on.

I want to be able to bring mums a listening ear, someone who's willing to step out of the books – willing to step out but not break the law, of course – someone who's willing to see you and your baby as an individual case. Our nannies are sensitive to cultural and religious differences, in addition to family traditions.

For example, I had a client who was from Indonesia. Her family members were making all of this food for her that was supposed to help her produce breast milk. I didn't have it in my script. They never taught me this at nanny school, but actually, when she ate the food that her mum cooked for her, she had lots of milk. It worked.

I want a nanny to be able to come in, taking into account the background of the person, look at the individual as an individual and be able to adapt what she knows and help this mum achieve what they want to achieve.

So apart from being able to do the nanny basics, nannies should be able to come in and look at every mum as an individual and empower those mums to do what they believe is right. I always say to the client, every baby is different, every mum is different. Women are completely different. Their views on what is right or what is wrong are going to be different, but here, they find themselves, they've had a child, and everyone is trying to apply some of the views they had.

Nannies come in, do their basic tasks, but should also listen to the mum and watch the baby and be able to adapt something that will work for the mum and for the baby.

I'll never forget being interviewed by a top nanny agency and them asking me what I wanted to do. I told them I wanted to empower women. The interviewer was supposed to ask me a set of questions but she says, "Oh, my God, that's what we really need. I'm about to be a mum, and if I could just find somebody who will help me to feel confident being a mum I will hire them and so would our clients. I should just jump onto it."

That means even mum-to-be, an agency doesn't want nannies who are just able to feed the baby, but they want nannies who are able to empower women because they know that's what will attract clients.

It takes a bit of adjustment for mothers to have this mindset. Some of them think, *Well, I've given you my money. Do your job.* They think of it with a business mindset. They don't expect me to encourage *them* to do it. And then find it even harder to admit they aren't sure. These are women who have high-powered, successful jobs. They don't want to admit they're stumped.

They say things like, "Winnie, I don't understand how this little thing here has had me so puzzled. I don't get it. Why can't I do it? I've dealt with big accounts and many of them. Why can't I handle this little thing right here?"

I tell them it's because they're two different things. Babies are not robots. It's not a robot that you slop the milk in, and you turn this button, and it should be sleeping because it's the time you expect them to be sleeping. That's not how babies work. This is a human being, and some of these mums are used to doing this by five o'clock, this by ten o'clock, and can't understand why the baby won't conform to this schedule. And they give up. They think they're doing it wrong, they think they've failed in some way.

This is what I believe is at the core of being an effective nanny. I want to go in and help them to understand that they are capable of adapting and using their natural skills to give their baby all the love and attention they need.

When hiring a nanny, I encourage parents to follow their instincts.

If a candidate comes to your home and she seems perfect on paper – she's on time, she has have a great CV and portfolio and trustworthy references, but your heart is still saying no, don't take her on. I tell many of my clients if for whatever reason you don't feel comfortable with me, don't hire me.

I believe as a nanny that I am there to help the mum – therefore if my presence has her trying to figure out why she is not at peace, she will be stressed not sleep and the baby will pick up on this. I have met mothers whose situation got worse when they got a nanny. These mothers felt they were not in control of their babies but only went along as spectators as the nanny did everything. They became stressed, with zero confidence.

A saying I use a lot is, "I don't buy stress." Mums who don't hire the perfect nanny may be worried sick. The ones who hire the perfect nanny are at peace – and empowered.

Your Partner Should Be in Your Corner

Before we start this section, I want to acknowledge the fact that not every woman, for any number of reasons, has a partner to help her with raising her children. The other sections in this chapter address asking for help from professionals and family and friends.

Traditionally, women are "supposed" to stay at home and take care of the kids. Luckily for modern women, times have changed and it is generally more acceptable for us to have jobs and lives outside of the home. But old habits die hard and even in today's society there is an underlying attitude that men should make the money and women should care for the children.

Sometimes this attitude is continued in our families by both men and women. A colleague of mine shared this story:

One night, when my son was about a month old, my husband offered to get up with him all night so I could sleep. It sounded great to me – until he woke up for the first time.

My husband got out of bed, picked him up, and I could hear him in the kitchen making a bottle. But the baby was still screaming. So there I lay, listening to all of this, wondering what he was doing wrong.

After a bit, I couldn't take it, so I sneaked down the hallway and peered around the corner. My husband caught me.

Later we laughed about it, but I remember him saying, "What's the point of both of us being up if you're going to be up no matter what?"

It wasn't until many years later, after our second child was born, that I realized I had taken some of the power away from my husband. I didn't let him figure things out on his own, I assumed my way was the only way, and I that I needed to handle everything. When I felt resentful that he didn't participate or care for the children more, or that I didn't get out much, I really had no one to blame but myself.

When I went on a business trip when our children were 6 and 3, and I had to lay out every single detail of the week so he wouldn't forget anything, I realized how much of a disservice I had done my family. My husband didn't feel capable and I was micromanaging everything. That trip taught all of us something that we should have known all along – he's a great father and can do everything that I can do as the mum.

Some men still feel that women should stay at home and, like in this story, some women perpetrate that stereotype themselves.

I say it's time for that attitude to end. Our partners should be just as involved in the lives of our children as we are. They should be able to care for them while mum works or goes out with her friends. It is a *partnership*.

Even in doing this project, my husband was saying that he wasn't sure if it was the right time for me to be doing this. I asked him, "Well when is the right time for me to be doing this?? I'm always going to have kids, they're always gonna be there. I think it's the perfect time for me to do this, because I am experiencing it as I'm going through and this is the right time for me to put down exactly what's happening. And if I talk to people, I can relate with them."

Some men feel threatened by successful women. They're afraid that at the end of the day it's going to take their wives away from the family. But that is not necessarily true. So we as empowered mums must, of course, respect our husbands but also stand up and say, get out of the way and let me do this!

The best way I've found to do this is keep my husband in the loop as much as possible when it comes to everything in our household. That includes the kids' schedules, where things are in the house, how to get them ready for school, etc.

I also make an effort to show him that I'm making time in our schedule for him. Of course it doesn't sound very romantic to say, "I've got time for you on Tuesday," but the important thing is that you make the time, however you can, to be together as husband and wife, not just mum and dad.

Who is in Your Village?

You have kids and kids frequently fall ill. Part of a working mum's guilt and stress comes from wondering what will happen when you have personal conflicts that affect your work. Like sick kids.

I've always told my sisters that before you have kids, create a network of people that you trust, that if anything happens to your child, you know that they can be taken care of if you can't be there immediately. I have three people; my mum, and my two sisters. I know I could pick up the phone and those three people would know everything about my kids. I have purposely told them everything about my kids.

For example, my daughter has viral-induced wheeze. What that basically means is that sometimes when she gets a cold, her breathing is affected and she can't breathe properly. So I need to be there to know what to do when that happens. But I realized, I can't be there all the time.

There was a time when she was getting sick every other week and I was working. If you're working and you're taking that much time off, obviously your employer is going to think, hold on, this is not really working.

So I invited my sister over and said, look, when Dorrinda falls ill, this is what you do – you call the doctor, etc. I put it on paper, but I also had her observe what happens so the next time it happened and they called me, guess who I called? I called my sister.

And she was even better than me. When you're a parent and your kids are ill, your emotions are all over the place and you're not thinking straight. But my sister was there and said, "Winnie, stay over there." The ambulance came and she told them everything – my daughter's date of birth, she was able to tell them that she is up to date with her immunizations, etc.

I have those other people as tools for my family. With them, I can be a great mum *and* a great working mum. If I was in the middle of an important meeting, I could finish that meeting, because I know there's somebody who is going to do exactly what I would do if I were there.

This is where women feel guilty. They're trying to do their jobs really well, but to let someone take over in an emergency may seem like you don't care about your kids. But you *do* care about your kids. You've made sure, before anything bad happens, that you have somebody who can take of your kids just as well as you can. Arm those people with the information that they need – your baby's date of birth, things they will need if there was a sickness situation, doctor's phone numbers, medicine dosages, etc. Remember that you're always just a phone call away. But you can prepare ahead of time – which makes you a dedicated, prepared, and *empowered* mum.

Chapter 6

Practical Application – Newborns

A colleague of mine told me this story about her experience after having her first baby:

Nine months felt like such a long time when I first found out I was pregnant. Then I was sick, I gained weight, I thought the baby was never going to come. Then all of a sudden my water broke and I was in the hospital and there was this very real, scary moment when I realized "Oh, no. This baby is coming out and I'm the only one who can do it and it's going to hurt!" It all seemed kind of abstract until I was actually there in the moment and it was all very overwhelming for me.

But then my son was born and, of course, I was overwhelmed by how much I loved him. I spent three days in the hospital and had a great experience. My nurses were great, I was sleeping well at night, and all I had to do was push a button when I had a question or got nervous about something and someone was there to help.

Then they started talking about discharge. Suddenly, I had another one of those very real moments. I remember thinking; "They're going to send me home with this baby?? Me?? What if I have a question? I don't know what I'm doing!"

I felt totally unprepared, even though I had been preparing for nine months.

As my husband and I loaded the baby in the car and drove home (about 20 miles an hour slower than we normally drive, with me turning around to check on the baby about 753 times), we were both in kind of a stunned silence. We had a baby. And now we had to figure out how to take care of that baby.

Obviously, once we got home, everything was fine. We got to know our son, figured out a routine, and gained confidence in the fact that we could love and care for our baby. It's just not something that anyone can explain to you.

I think this experience is common in new mums. When you're pregnant you can do everything possible to prepare; read books, do internet research, and get advice from doctors and friends. But when a nurse hands you your baby for the first time, all you can think about is everything you *don't* know.

After all, babies don't come with a manual. There's no way of knowing if your baby will have colic, if he'll like to be swaddled or not, if he'll prefer a dummy. It can feel overwhelming and sometimes even impossible.

But it's *not* impossible. Babies can be difficult to figure out, but their needs aren't complicated. It may take a lot of trial and error – you may need to try different bottles, dummies, schedules, etc., before you find what works for you and your baby. But remember, that *you* are the expert when it comes to your baby. You are capable of taking care of your baby and, most importantly, giving your baby the love and attention he needs.

The most important thing to remember with your newborn is that all you have to do is feed him, change him, and love him. You and your baby are still getting to know each other – be gentle with yourself and *do what works for your baby.* Your baby is a unique individual – what works for your friends' babies may not work for yours.

Now, none of this means that you shouldn't ask for help! You can use other people's experience and advice to help you figure out what the options are for you and your baby. Maybe you'd never considered using gas drops or a swaddle or a sound machine, and they all turn out to be great techniques for calming your baby.

In this chapter, I've combined my best tips and tricks for taking care of newborns. Some of these I've used with my own kids and others I've used through my experience as a nanny.

In the last chapter of this book, we'll have a list of further resources for you.

Sleep

This is probably the number one question I get from new mums – *When will I ever sleep again??* Unfortunately, there is no simple answer. Some babies sleep through the night by three months old, others at 6 months when they are on solid foods, or others not until they're older! It simply depends on your baby's needs and there is no quick fix.

Why don't babies just sleep like normal people?

Newborns sleep about 16-17 hours a day – which sounds like a lot! But a baby's sleep cycle is shorter than that of an adult's. They spend more time in REM (rapid eye movement) sleep than adults, which is believed to be vital for the rapid development occurring in their brain. REM sleep is a "lighter" sleep, which means that babies are more easily awakened.

Another factor working against you is that newborns can sometimes have their days and nights confused or they need to be fed and changed frequently.

All of this means that those 16-17 hours of sleep come in two to four increments, making it difficult for mums to catch any solid stretch of rest. It is the irregular and interrupted sleep that exhausts new parents.

This also means that until your baby grows out of this stage of development, he won't be able to be on a regular schedule – it's just something you have to get through.

At 6-8 weeks, these patterns start to change. Babies begin to sleep less during the day and for longer stretches at night (although they will still wake up to be fed – it just becomes a bit less frequent and slightly more predictable).

So what can you do? Fortunately, there are some effective ways for preparing your baby to establish healthy sleeping patterns, even before they move out of the newborn stage.

Start a routine. Every baby is different, so just establish a routine that works for your family. It may be bathing, nursing/bottle, then bed. Or reading, nursing/bottle, singing a song, then bed. Just follow the same routine whenever possible. As the baby gets older, he will learn to associate this routine with bedtime.

Teach Self-soothing. Putting baby in her crib when she is sleepy, but before she actually falls asleep will teach her how to fall asleep alone and how to soothe herself if she should wake up in the middle of the night. An important part of this strategy is to watch for signs that baby is tired. If she is rubbing her eyes or being fussy when there isn't something else wrong, it may be because she's tired. Laying her down when you notice those signs will teach her that being tired means laying down.

It's important to note that not all parents and experts agree with this strategy. Some parents prefer to rock their babies to sleep. Remember – what's most important is that you do what's best for your family.

Teach Day and Night. When baby is awake during the day, play and interact with him as much as possible. Keep the shades open and lights on and don't intentionally minimize regular noises such as the phone, television, or vacuum.

When he does wake at night, be "all business." Feed and change him, give him some cuddles, and then it's back to bed. This way he will learn that, when it's dark, he's expected to go back to sleep.

The most important thing to remember about babies and sleep is that they won't be waking you up three (or four or five!) times a night forever. But they're not *supposed* to sleep through the night right away. It's simply a stage of their development that you have to get through. Of course, some babies are simply divine, like my son who from day one would sleep from 8pm to 8am. However, when my first daughter was born she was up almost every 2 hours. Every baby is different. What's important is that you learn effective ways to deal with the exhaustion and enjoy your baby.

Here are some things you can do to combat the exhaustion that comes along with having a newborn:

Sleep when baby sleeps. Whenever possible, catch a nap when the baby is sleeping. You may be tempted to fold laundry or clean the kitchen, but that can wait. Getting some rest is much more important.

Ask for help. Ask your partner or a trusted family member or friend to take care of baby so you can sleep for an extended period of time. It's amazing how much better you will feel with four or five hours of uninterrupted sleep! If you can afford it, arrange for a Night Nanny, who will care for the baby through the whole night.

Take a break. Sometimes babies just refuse to sleep or they won't stop crying. If you're sleep-deprived the sound of a crying baby can be stressful and cause feelings of anxiety and even anger. If you feel yourself getting to that point, *take a break.* Make sure your baby is safe and all of his needs are met – full belly, clean nappy, safe place to lay him down – and walk into the next room or even sit on the porch outside. It will not hurt your baby to cry alone for a couple of minutes while you compose yourself. A more calm and patient parent will help both of you.

Breastfeeding v. Formula Feeding

This is one area in which mothers are very, very judgmental of each other. I want to say right away that that most important thing is for you to do what is best for you and your baby. *Every family is different.*

The science is clear; breastfeeding is nutritionally best for babies. But that doesn't mean it's always the easiest or healthiest option.

There are many reasons why a new mum might not choose to breastfeed at all or only for a short time:

- She has to take medication that is passed through her breast milk but is harmful to baby.

- She doesn't produce enough milk.

- She has to return to work.

- The baby has to spend time in the Special Care Baby Unit after birth and is required to be fed via bottle.

However you choose to feed your baby, whether it's exclusive breastfeeding, pumping breast milk and feeding via bottle, or formula feeding, as long as your baby is healthy and thriving, that is all that matters.

In this section I want to provide you with some helpful tricks about feeding baby, no matter how you choose to do so.

Breastfeeding

Breastfeeding is the "natural" way to feed babies. It provides babies with all the essential nutrients they need for health, in addition to fostering a deep bond between baby and mum. However, that doesn't mean that it comes naturally to all mums. Breastfeeding can be difficult and painful. New mums can get frustrated by being the only one who can feed the baby and the stress of not knowing exactly how much food the baby is getting.

Hundreds of books have been written about breastfeeding, and there is entirely too much information out there to include in this book. However, here are my favourite tips and tricks for breastfeeding your baby successfully:

Prepare to breastfeed. Even before your baby is born, prepare yourself mentally to breastfeed. You can read books, speak to other mothers, or seek out advice from a professional. If you have had a baby before and your milk supply was not great the first time, this time you can find out in advance how you can increase your supply and address any other issues that you struggled with when nursing your first baby.

When I had my first born, my milk supply was okay and I was able to breastfeed for six months. When baby number two was born it was the opposite: I had no milk, I was constantly stressed, and eventually gave up earlier than I wanted to. When baby three came along, I did a combination of breast and bottle, but then she preferred the bottle and refused the breast. With baby number four, I did not leave anything to chance. I prepared by getting a breast pump so that even if the baby would only feed from the bottle it was breast milk. During the feeds when the other children were in school and nursery I breastfed. This way the baby knew what to expect at different feeds and this was more successful for me.

DO NOT compare yourself to others. We are all different, with difference bodies, experiences, and we live in different environments. The most important thing is that you do what works for YOU – not what worked for a friend or your mother or anyone else.

DO NOT over think it. Do not allow yourself to over complicate breastfeeding. Your body is designed to do this naturally. Ask yourself how often during the week you sit down and figure out how to breathe? You don't – you just do it naturally. Let breastfeeding be the same. Let baby latch on and feed. If you feel thirsty during feeding, drink a glass of water. When the baby is finished, continue with your day remembering to eat regularly. There is nothing wrong with preparing to breastfeed – but it is natural. You don't have to read every single book or prepare for every possible scenario. Let your body do what it's made to do.

Enjoy it. During the feeding, relax. Forget the housework for an hour and watch and observe your baby. I found at these times I tuned in more to my baby and she was happy to stay even longer, resulting in a better feed and helped us avoid her snacking during the day.

Ask for help. Whether it's help from your spouse at nursing time or help from a family member or friend so that you can take a break, don't be afraid to ask. You should also take advantage of your doctor's knowledge. They are there to help you with any questions you have and can also point you in the direction of a lactation consultant.

Find the position that works for you. There are four main positions for breastfeeding; cross-over, football, side-lying, and cradle. Not every mum enjoys all of them. Try them all out and decide which works best for you.

Breast-Feeding Positions

Cradle hold

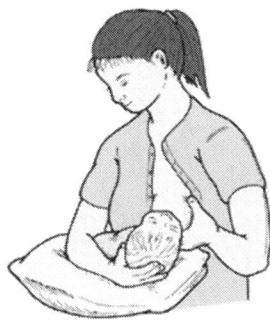

Cross-cradle hold

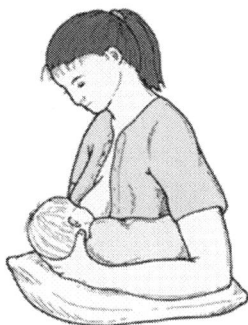

Football hold

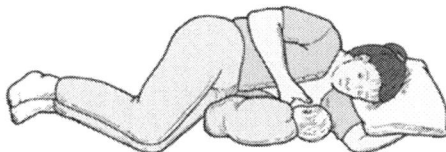

Lying down

Relax. While nursing, find a comfortable spot, keep the room dim and quiet, and focus on your baby. Try to think of it as a time to relax and get away from the chaos of daily life. This will not only help your milk production, but it will also help calm your baby and strengthen your bond.

Take notes. Keep track of how long and on which side you feed the baby. This will not only help you keep track of how much baby is eating, but will also help in the future for creating – and sticking to – a schedule.

Talk to other mums. If you have friends who have successfully breastfed their babies, ask what worked for them. Every woman addresses feeding issues differently and they may have some tricks you haven't thought of yet.

Formula Feeding

Formula feeding provides your baby with all of the essential nutrition a baby needs. It also allows both mum and dad to take an active part in feeding. However, formula feeding can be expensive and it sometimes takes a lot of trial and error to figure out which formula is best for your baby.

Combined with advice from your paediatrician, the following list of tips will be able to help you formula feed successfully.

Ask for samples. Your doctor or hospital should have samples of various formulas on hand. If the current formula you're using doesn't seem to sit well with the baby, using samples will allow you to try different kinds without spending a lot of money on whole containers of formula.

Take notes. Just like with breastfeeding, keeping track of how long and how much you feed the baby will help you keep track of how much the baby is eating, and will also help in the future for creating – and sticking to – a schedule.

Relax. Formula feeding can help you form just as deep a bond as breastfeeding. When it's time to feed baby, keep the room quiet and dim and focus on baby. If possible, get skin-to-skin contact with your baby.

Milestones

The below milestones are simply guidelines to give you a general idea of what your baby should be able to do and can be used to check your baby's progress at each stage of development.

But it's important to remember that every baby develops differently. Some babies will reach milestones early and some will be a little behind. If you are concerned about your baby's development, it's important to speak with your baby's paediatrician and follow his or her advice.

The following list is adapted from healthychildren.org, from the American Academy of Paediatrics.

From 3 months, your baby should be able to:

- Raises head & chest when on stomach

- Stretches & kicks on back

- Opens and shuts hands

- Brings hand to mouth

- Grasps and shakes toys

- Begins to develop social smile

- Enjoys playing with people

- More communicative

- More expressive with face & body

- Imitates some movements & expressions

- Follows moving objects

- Recognizes familiar objects and people at a distance

- Starts using hands and eyes in coordination

- Prefers sweet smells

- Prefers soft to coarse sensations

Chapter 7

Practical Application –

3 Months – 1 Year

After three months, your baby will develop into the chubby, smiley baby of your dreams. Your baby's personality will start to shine through – she will make it clear if she doesn't like lying on her tummy, or loves peaches, or would prefer to face out and see the world. This stage of development is so much fun – all of the exhaustion and stress of the first months will seem well worth it the first time your baby smiles or giggles at you.

But it's not without its challenges. As your baby becomes more aware of his surroundings, he will start to exert his independence – sometimes very loudly! You will also face new challenges such as teething, starting solid foods, and getting baby on a schedule.

Sleeping Through the Night

Most babies will be ready to sleep through the night – at a stretch of 8-12 hours – somewhere between four and six months. Some will continue to wake in the middle of the night into toddlerhood – but there are some ways to help your baby learn to love sleep.

Take Notes. Most mothers have trouble figuring out why baby is still waking up in the night. They always ask me, "What can I do?" I love such babies because I love a challenge, and I love the mum's face when I tell them I can guarantee within a week, their baby will be able to sleep until the morning. They don't believe me. "But how, when?" and then I say to them, "Here's a piece of paper. I want you to write down for the next week how much food your baby eats, when the baby eats, when the baby sleeps, what the baby does during the day –everything.

Then I look at the records they've made, and I always I see a pattern. There are few reasons why babies will wake up in the night. They're going to wake up if they're too cold or if they're too hot. They're going to wake up if they're hungry and they may even wake up if they need their nappy to be changed. Usually, it's because the baby is not getting enough food in the day. That's why they're waking up in the night, to eat.

Most of those issues you can address immediately, so any long-term problems usually relate to feeding. So I'll come in and say, "Okay. I want to just make sure you feed the baby at this time and that time and that time and feed them this amount of food." That way I know when I get there at night, the baby has had enough food to eat in the day. When that happens, baby will almost always start sleeping through the night.

Cry it Out. This is a controversial topic. And I understand that nobody likes to hear the baby cry. Actually, *I* hate letting babies cry, and this is what I do for a living! Most of the time, I pray, please let the mum do it herself because I don't want to let babies to cry!

But I also believe it is the most effective way to help a baby learn to sleep through the night. If a baby is upset and waking during the night and it's clear that it's not due to being hungry, having a dirty nappy, or some other issue, they are probably waking during the night out of habit. The baby's going to go back to sleep as soon as they realize that they do not want to be awake. You can train your baby to just go back to sleep.

There are gentle ways of helping the baby to stop crying... Experts say it takes between four to five days for a baby to learn something new, so that's why I say, I guarantee, within four to five days, I can teach a baby how to do it.

I think the best way to illustrate this point is to tell a story. I had a mother who called me for nanny services. It was several weeks before I actually went in. She seemed like she wasn't sure whether she wanted me to come in and help. I assured her that I only wanted to come when she was ready for the help because I wanted her to be ready to listen. Half the time, the baby is ready, but if the mother's not ready to implement what you're going to tell them, it's never going to work. I assure the mums to try everything they can think of before I come in. So once this mum was ready, off I went.

This mum, she'd had it up to here. The baby was waking up every two hours in the night, every night. We sat around the table, and I said, "Okay. So tell me about this." They told me the baby started to wake up about 10:30-ish. Sure enough, as we were sitting at the table, 10:30 came around and all of a sudden, their faces just changed. I said, "What's wrong?" They responded, "Oh, no, she's starting."

I couldn't even hear anything at first, so I said, "Starting what?" Then I heard it - the baby was just making little noises, a little "A-huh, a-huh," not really crying, just making that noise.

So I told the parents to sit down. I said, "You call that crying? That's not crying. That baby's just whimpering. She's not crying." I said, "Sit down."

They weren't talking and mum said "Oh, my God, can you ..." and started to get upset. I told her to sit down again, that it would be fine. I turned on the timer on my phone for ten minutes and kept talking.

After fifteen minutes, the baby was still making those noises, but the baby was still not actually crying.

After twenty minutes, mum still wanted to go in. I encouraged her not to. I said, "The baby's not crying, so there's no point in you going 'cause the baby's not crying. She's just making some noises."

After thirty minutes, they looked at me and said, "We don't care. We're going to go in."

I asked them for five more minutes and told them that after five minutes, they could go to her door – but could not go into the bedroom. I told them just to peek in through the door, and make sure the baby didn't have anything over her face, that she was securely tucked in, and nothing was obstructing her airway.

So they went and looked. I literally went with them, saying, "Do not go into the room, do not turn the lights on." Normally they were rushing in, picking up the baby, and fully waking the baby up.

I asked if they were satisfied that the baby was safe. They said yes, but were still upset that she was "crying." I said, "She's not crying. Close the door. Go on back to the sitting room."

Twenty minutes after that, she stopped and they were amazed. I said, "Yeah. Of course, she's not crying. She's not hungry. You just showed me when you fed her, so it's not food, it's not heat, it's none of those. She's used to waking up and you rushing in and doing what you just did."

That was day one. After just that scenario, I was booked for the whole week. She never woke up in the middle of the night again. So this baby was a really clever baby. Just after that 30 minutes or 40 minutes, I let the baby supposedly cry as far as they were concerned. But this baby never started doing that noise again, and never again woke up every two hours.

The baby never went back to that previous routine of crying every two hours again. This mum is now a great advocate of mine. She's brought me so many clients because she believes I'm a miracle worker, but I'm not really. Because I was able to say, "Actually, no, the baby is fine."

Sometimes babies will relapse and go back to waking up for whatever reason as they're growing, and they'll have growth spurts, and they'll need to be fed more food, but I always make sure I leave my clients empowered so that if this ever happens again, they will know what to do. And they always bring their friends to me.

Keep it consistent. Sticking to a bedtime routine alerts baby that it's time for bed – whether it's bath, story, then bed, or singing songs, saying prayers, then bed, do whatever works. This helps your baby wind down and allows sleep to take over. If you consistently do the same thing the baby will come to expect it, thereby learning this is what we do at night and will repeat the same every night.

Getting Baby on Schedule

I've got four kids, and unfortunately, let's just say, my husband is not able right now to take care of everything. But I need to be able to go to work *and* take care of my kids, just like all mums. If a mum wants to have a career (or even just keep her house clean and presentable and get dinner on the table at night!), the key to doing that successfully is having a routine.

Nannies can help families do this. Believe it or not, babies and kids love a routine.

Take advantage of naps. When baby naps – and they sleep the longest in the afternoon, between twelve and two – a mum can organize herself, whether that means work or making phone calls, you can get a lot done when the baby is quiet.

Peace of Mind. If you work and you know what your baby is doing at all times throughout the day, you'll be in a better place to concentrate. If I didn't know my babies were fine throughout the day and what they were doing, I would be so distracted, that I wouldn't be very effective.

Babies love a routine because they know at this time, I'm expecting my drink, at this time, I'm expecting this, so the baby's happy, you're happy, everybody's happy, but it's just having somebody there to show you how to do that. Nannies can do that.

Many times, mums ask me, "Winnie, how can you do this [work nights]? You've got a six-month-old baby." I can do this because I know exactly what my six-month-old baby is doing at midnight, at one o'clock, at two o'clock. I know exactly what they're doing. For example if I was to pick up my phone say at 3am (in my experience many babies wake up at this hour) and call home, and I hear the baby in the background, I will know something's not quite right because she sleeps soundly through the night.. Knowing my baby sleeps through until 8 am gives me peace of mind allowing me to focus at work and helps me feel in control and takes away a lot of the stress of being away from home.

Teething

Teething babies are a challenge – it lasts for a while, they can't tell you what is wrong, and it can cause a baby to regress in some of their milestones because they just don't feel good. It can be a stressful time for parents and babies.

Teething usually starts between four to seven months. Usually, babies get the two front teeth, on either top or bottom, first. It may be weeks between when you first notice symptoms (pain at night, swollen gums, general fussiness, excessive drooling) and when you actually see the teeth emerge.

Any experienced mum will have their own secrets to combat teething. Here are a few of my favourites:

- Teething tablets

- Frozen teethers

- Ibuprofen (when necessary, with doctor's approval)

Me Time

It is expected of the mum at this stage of the baby's life to solely focus on the baby; this is true and to many mums it comes as second nature. What I have found is how rarely mums will schedule any time for themselves away from the baby. I have found that those that do take time out for themselves sometimes spent half that time feeling guilty for being away from their baby. When I talk about time I don't mean taking weeks away from the baby; rather, this takes place on a daily basis schedule in thirty minutes intervals in the home, and an hour, or two hours where you have arranged for someone you trust to care for the baby while you go out. During this 'me time', do something you enjoy or did before you had the baby; go to the gym, meet with friends, anything that you enjoy doing.

Having four children make it a challenge for me to have my 'me time', but I know if I don't have it, I feel like I'm on a treadmill and can never get off. This can only last for so long before you reach breaking point and in turn everyone around you will know about it. You may feel guilty for the first few times but keep it up; your baby and the rest of the family will love the new, rested you.

Milestones

The below milestones are simply guidelines to give you a general idea of what your baby should be able to do and can be used to check your baby's progress at each stage of development.

But it's important to remember that every baby develops differently. Some babies will reach milestones early and some will be a little behind. If you are concerned about your baby's development, it's important to speak with your baby's paediatrician and follow his or her advice.

The following list is adapted from healthychildren.org, from the American Academy of Paediatrics.

From 4-7 months, your baby should be able to:

- Rolls both ways

- Sits with and without support of hands

- Supports whole weight on legs

- Reaches with one hand

- Transfers object from hand to hand

- Uses raking grasp

- Enjoys social play

- Interested in mirror images

- Responds to expressions of emotion

- Appears joyful often

- Finds partially hidden object

- Explores with hands and mouth

- Struggles to get objects that are out of reach

From 8-12 months, your baby should be able to:

- Gets to sitting position without help

- Crawls forward on belly

- Assumes hands-and-knees position

- Gets from sitting to crawling position

- Pulls self up to stand

- Walks holding on to furniture

- Shy or anxious with strangers

- Cries when parents leave

- Enjoys imitating people in play

- Prefers certain people and toys

- Tests parental response

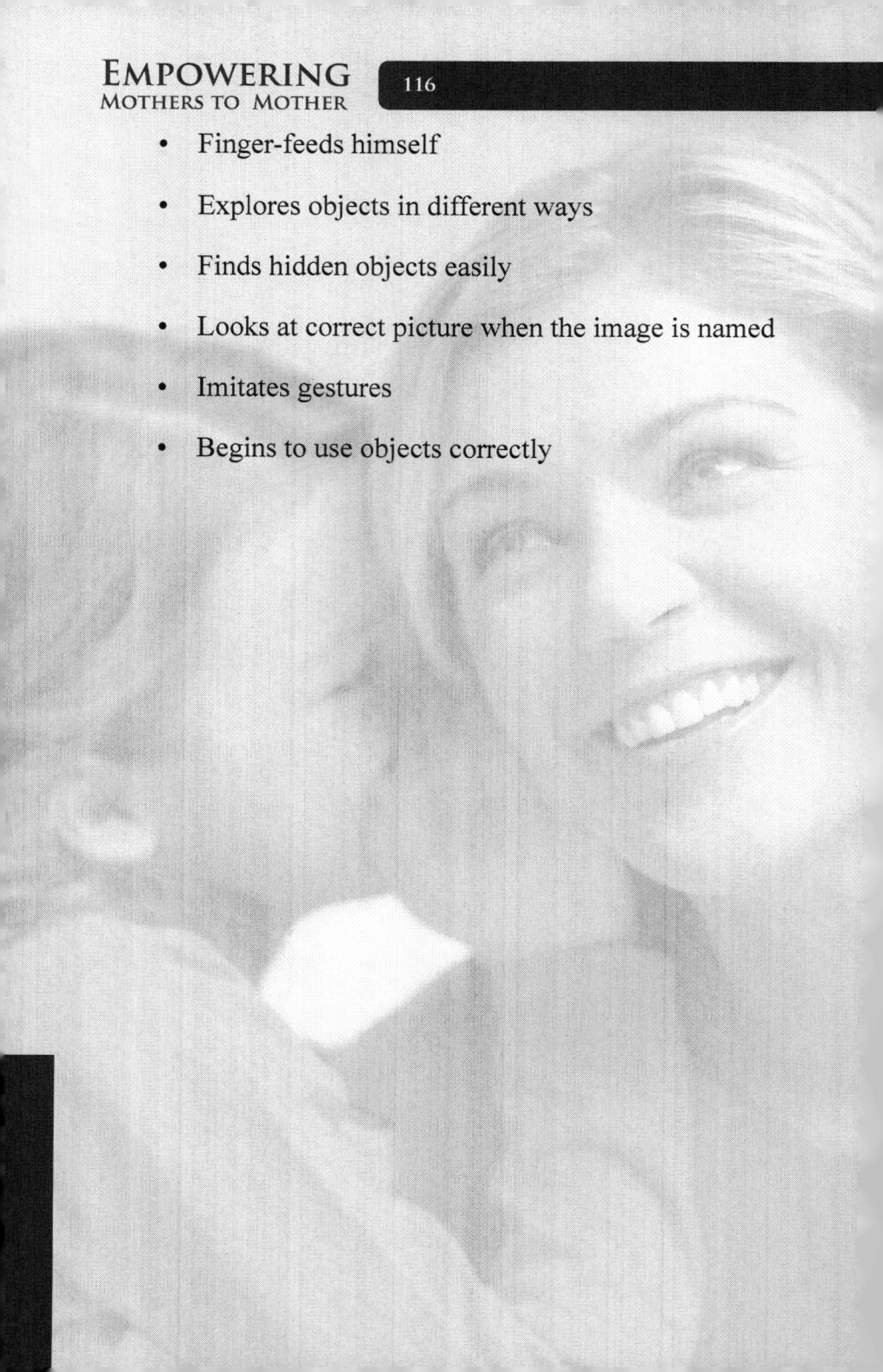

- Finger-feeds himself

- Explores objects in different ways

- Finds hidden objects easily

- Looks at correct picture when the image is named

- Imitates gestures

- Begins to use objects correctly

Chapter 8

Practical Application –
One Year and Beyond

After your baby turns one, they are officially a toddler. While this makes many new mums sad, it's also an opportunity to really get to know your child as a person. Their personality shines through and as they learn to talk, it's amazing to hear their ideas about the world and see their creative sides come through.

Challenges you will face as the parent of a toddler include teaching independence (while keeping the baby safe!), introducing another baby, and helping them understand complicated ideas about the world around them.

The Importance of Independence

I do have a nanny that helps me with my children – I cannot overstate the value that I believe nannies do have. But it's important to me that our nanny allows my children to teach them to do things for themselves. My kids help with the washing and are learning how to bathe themselves. My nanny couldn't believe that I was going to let my three-year-old bathe herself. I simply told my daughter, "Okay. There's the shower. Here's the cloth. You put the soap on it."

Even if she's not clean at the end, it doesn't matter. What's important is that I'm letting her do it. Many nannies would think, *oh, this is taking too long. It's just quicker if I do it myself.* But that doesn't help the child learn.

Teaching independence is vital to a child's development. Not only does allowing a child do things alone teach vital life skills, but it also helps develop confidence. Children will learn the importance of responsibility and looking after themselves.

Much like helping mums, this independence empowers our children. They realize that we, as parents, trust them to do things. There is a reason kids constantly say, "I do it myself, do it myself." They are capable and willing to learn new things.

As parents, we have a long list of responsibilities – we have to work, pay bills, do laundry, it's endless. We can't monitor our kids every second of every day. It's absolutely necessary that we teach them to meet some of their own needs.

For example, I've taught my kids that when we go to bed, it means we stay in bed, and we sleep unless you want to go to toilet. If you do need to go, get up, go to the toilet, and go back to bed. If I hadn't disciplined them to be able to sleep properly until the morning, and they keep waking up, monkeying around all throughout the night, I'm not going to be able to work because I'm going to be tired, worried that the nanny won't be able to deal with them, etc. But my kids do know how to handle themselves, so I have the confidence that when I go to work, I know exactly what my kids are doing.

Teaching independence also helps our children learn to think for themselves and draw their own conclusions about the world around them. I've been telling my son, "Look, TV's not good for you." "Yeah, but, Mummy, but why?" I just said, "It's not good for you. Because every time I ask you a question, if you're watching TV, I'll be calling you and calling you, but if you're concentrating on the TV, you can't hear me speak."

After two weeks without him watching intensive TV he said, "Mummy, I think I understand now what you mean by TV's bad for you because if a teacher asks you what's one plus one, you're going to say Auggie and the Cockroaches because you've been watching them, and that's what you're thinking about, so your brain's not quickly thinking about the answer, so it's going to slow you down." I was like, oh, thank God he's got it!

I believe that in modern society, in the developed world, we don't give our children as much opportunity to do things for themselves. Obviously, society is different now; most children don't have to gather water to bring to the house or feed animals on a farm or quit school at 12 years old in order to go to work to support their family. But there is value in those things. As parents, we need to keep an open mind and learn not only from the influences in our own lives, but from those people whose lives and cultures are drastically different than ours.

I remember this story a colleague told me about how different parenting styles in different parts of the world have a lot to teach us.

I was visiting family in Uganda and my niece, who was three at the time, was getting ready to take a bath. I watched her run the water, get the soap, get all her towels, and get everything ready. The whole time I'm thinking, my daughter, who was five at the time, would have never done that. She would have been waiting for us to get everything ready for her.

When my niece was done, she even put lotion on, asking for help with her back, and then put everything away.

When I returned home from that trip, I gave my daughter one week to learn how to wash herself. She was indignant at first, but I told her, "You're using a better shower, she's using a really very complicated little bath. Please, it's not even negotiable. She is three, you are five. My wife even argued and said that she will start bathing herself when she was seven, but I said nope, she's got a week.

Sure enough, she learned within a week. And for my daughter it was the most empowering thing. From that day forward, she was always really excited and proud to do it herself.

Consistency

As my children get older, I am finding it equally as essential as when they were babies to have consistency and routine. Here are a few things that I keep consistent in my home:

Meals. Having structured meals allows us to connect to each other as a family; we can discuss our day, our schedule for the next day, and generally touch base. This also provides a good marker for all of your schedules; your kids will know when to be home from a friend's house or your spouse will be able to schedule meetings around family dinners. It's also a chance for you to provide healthy and nutritious meals.

Nap time. Until my children were two and attending nursery, I made sure they napped at the same time every day. Not only did this help me schedule our days, but it also helped with them sleeping well at night; if they skipped a nap they were often overly tired by bedtime and had difficulty getting to sleep.

Bedtime. A consistent bedtime not only helps with kids getting all the sleep they need to stay healthy, but it also allows mum and dad some quiet time at night. A bedtime routine signals to the kids it's time to quieten down, to slow down, and minimizes repeated calls for drinks, bathroom breaks, help with their blankets, and all of the other very creative excuses kids come up with to delay bedtime.

Weekly activities. It can be difficult to manage several different schedules. With swimming, going to the park, sports, etc., your family may feel as though they're spending all of their time away from home. If you schedule activities at the same time, when possible, not only does it alleviate some of the stress of figuring out who needs to be where and when, but it also allows you to schedule time to spend as a family, for homework, and for relaxing.

You will find, at this stage, children have a lot of energy and keeping up with them – especially when you have 2, 3, or 4 children – can seem like a losing battle. With a routine or time table of what you do from 6am/7am to 6pm/7am, you will know exactly what you need to do, which in turn will encourage you to be prepared and plan your days, weeks, and months. It is especially important during school holidays, when kids are transitioning from the structure of school or nursery.

Many times I will start an activity with the children, say painting, and 20 minutes into the activity they are already asking me, "What are we doing next mum?" It's great that your child is keen to do a lot, but sometimes if you have not planned in advance it can become stressful for you trying to come up with ideas on the spot.. Having a time table keeps you one step ahead so that before you start the day you can tell the children what they are going to do that day.

When writing the timetable get the children involved. Use pictures – show them that this is fun. This way, you will raise children who will grow up with planning and being organized as a part of their life rather than a skill they have to learn when they are older.

Let your yes be yes and your no be no.

Every mother wants to have a child who is well behaved, especially when you go out or are visiting friends and family.

When I went to my daughter's stay and play session at her new nursery, it was interesting to watch the other parents interact with their kids. You could immediately tell which parents allowed their children to get away with whatever they wanted at home because the child would cry, vomit, or fall on the floor in the middle of the supermarket and refuse to get up until they got their way. These parents desperately wanted little Sally to share with the other children, but just like at home, she wanted her way. The mum would feel so embarrassed and the look on her face, begging the child to behave, said it all.

It is easy when you are tired to give in to what the children want, but always ask yourself; *what am I teaching my child?* Don't wait for the nursery to teach your child – start at home.

I come from a big family with three sisters and two brothers. One day I asked my mum "How did you manage to keep us in line when they were six of us?" She replied "Let your yes be yes and your no be no."

When I asked her what she meant, she said, "Well, if you tell your child, if you don't do as you're told, I'm going to throw you out the window. Well, that's not realistic because you're not going to throw them out the window. You're not going to throw them out the window, so they're going to think, whatever, Mummy's just always says that to scare us, there won't be any real consequences if I don't listen."

You have to show your children that there will be consequences for their actions.

I use this all the time with my own kids. For instance I believe in eating together at the dining table without the TV. Many times my son will ask me "Mummy could we have a day off and watch TV?" My answer is always no, but this does not stop him from asking me several times during the week. It would be easy to say yes, especially when he has been a good boy, but I remind myself the importance of the family eating together and I say no. Eventually he realizes mum is not going to change; now he tells his sisters to turn the TV off.

My mother was an amazing woman – she took care of six kids and provided a great life for us. Part of what made her so wonderful was the fact that she disciplined us when we needed it – she wasn't too harsh, but we always learned our lesson.

For example, one of my chores was washing up after dinner. I remember one time after dinner she told me, "Go and do the washing up." This was at 5:00 p.m. and I remember thinking, *I'm not doing the washing up. I'm not going to do any washing up. I'm going to my room.* And I didn't do it.

But mum would just tell us something once, so she didn't mention it for the rest of that evening. She kept quiet, and I went to sleep thinking, *I've got away with this.* But I kid you not, at 3:00 a.m. in the morning, she came in and woke me up. My first thought was, *what's wrong?* But she just said, "did you do the washing up?" and I remember thinking, *What? Did I do the washing up? It's 3:00 a.m. in the morning. I'm sleeping!*

Very calmly, not shouting, but in an assertive way, she said, "Get up now and go and do the washing up." I knew she meant get up right then and go and do the washing up. So there I was, at 3:00 a.m., screaming and crying and complaining, saying all the words under the planet, but I went downstairs, stood by that sink, and did the washing up. I guarantee you after that, I always did the washing up at five o'clock.

Having Another Baby – and Helping Siblings Cope

Involve the whole family. Every time I meet with a new client and they learn I am a mother of four, their first question is "How do you do it?"

When I learned I was going to have baby number four, I prepared the children by involving them in everything, up until my daughter was born. I would let them listen to the baby, feel the baby move, ask their opinion about names, take them shopping for the baby, and let them chose some of the clothes. When the baby arrived, it wasn't just mummy's baby it was *our* baby and they enjoyed helping me to look after the baby.

It's natural to be very protective of the baby and easier to tell siblings to stay away. I find this makes the children feel second best and as though someone is taking their place with mum. This is when they start to act up and start to seek attention. Once the baby is fed or asleep, make time to spend with the other children.

Be organized. With more than one child it's a must to be organized. This way you don't miss things and you can schedule time for all children, rather than leaving it to chance. It's also important to schedule breaks for yourself as, with more than one child, you are in high demand. Combined with no rest or sleep, every task may seem like a mountain climb.

It's important to schedule time for each child even if it's just 30 minutes each, this way every child has a special bond with you and does not feel left out.

When you start feeling guilty that you are not spending enough time with the other children but rather feel like you are mostly with the baby, stop and ask yourself the following questions:

- What is top priority now? Your priorities will change as the baby grows, but in the first two weeks both you and baby are the priority as the baby needs to feed and you need the rest to be able to feed the baby. During these weeks get as much help as you can; if Dad is on paternity leave, let him help and ask grandparents, friends, and a night nanny if you can.

- How much time are you really spending with the baby and the other siblings? This is where having a timetable will help because you will know in advance when you are with the baby and when you are with the other children.

Empowering Mothers to Mother

- What can I do to balance the time spent between the baby and the other children? When you identify what time is truly spent with the baby and the other children, if one seems to be getting more than the other, adapt the timetable to address it. You may find that you regularly need to adapt your timetable to accommodate your children's and baby's changing needs.

- Lastly, make a plan to do it and STOP feeling guilty.

Potty Training

Perhaps one of the most dreaded of all parenting tasks is also the messiest – potty training. I've spoken with countless mums who all have a different experience – some children are easy to train, others take months, others still aren't interested at all.

Just like with breastfeeding, sleeping, and just about everything else, no single potty training solution will work for every mum or child. What often works in the end is a combination of advice from books, the internet, other parents, and some intuition.

One thing is for sure – while messy and frustrating potty training can also provide some of the funniest parenting moments. And if we can't laugh about it, we might as well cry. So before we dive into some practical tips to help you and your little one say goodbye to nappies, I thought I'd share some funny potty training stories from friends, colleagues, and my own kids.

When we decided that we were ready to start potty training my son, we weren't sure how to go about it. So I went out and bought the "Potty Time Elmo" DVD, along with a big boy potty that I let him pick out. As soon as we got home, he wanted to watch the movie. As soon as I turned it on, he quickly ran down the hallway, only to return immediately with his potty. We decided we weren't going to push him too hard, so for the next couple of weeks, he would watch the DVD over and over (and over and over again), but only if he could sit on his potty, in the living room. The only problem was that he wasn't actually using the potty for its intended purpose. One day I moved the potty back into the bathroom, took his diaper off, and let him sit. Lo and behold, he used the potty properly and after only about a week, he was fully trained. I give all the credit to Elmo. And I'll never forget the image of him sitting in the living room, on the potty.

When we were potty training my daughter, she had a hard time sitting still on the potty long enough for anything to happen. So I made up a silly song that I would use to distract her while we were waiting. Unfortunately, before long she wanted me to sing this song every single time, no matter where we were. She had to use the potty one day while we were at the store and sure enough, she asked me to sing the song. I didn't think anyone was in the restroom with us, so I did. When she was done, she proudly described exactly what she had accomplished. When we walked out of the stall, I was mortified to see a woman standing there, washing her hands. Not only had she heard my daughter's lovely exclamation, but also my song.

My son was about 3 and had recently been potty trained. We were still working on mastering, how shall I say, how all of his "parts" worked. We were out at a restaurant one day and he needed to use the bathroom. My brother was with us, and he wanted his uncle to take him. My brother reluctantly agreed. A few minutes later, they returned to the table and my brother did not look pleased. I asked what happened. He said, "Well. I thought he could go to the bathroom standing up. Turns out he can, but when I asked him a question, he didn't just turn his head – he turned his whole body. While he was still going. It went everywhere.*" I tried to contain my laughter, but I have to admit, I couldn't.*

Potty training can be a difficult task and there are thousands of sources for advice, from books that claim you can potty train in one day, to potty training boot camps, and even those that claim you can potty train a baby. It can be overwhelming to try to figure out what will work for your child.

I've compiled a list of the techniques I've found worked best, either for my children or for other parents. It will take a lot of trial and error, but eventually you'll find a system that works for your family.

Wait until they're ready. Experts agree that children are generally ready for potty training when they exhibit all or some of the following signs:

- ✓ Ask questions about mum, dad, or siblings using the potty or toilet.

- ✓ Their nappy stays dry through nap and/or bedtime.

- ✓ They inform you when they're going or when their diaper is dirty.

- ✓ The number of dirty nappies decreases; essentially, they "go" more at one time.

- ✓ Complains about a dirty nappy.

- ✓ Is walking, can pull their pants up and down, and can follow simple instruction.

It's important not to start potty training before a child is ready. If they're not physically or cognitively ready, the process will be very frustrating both for the child and his parents. It's understandable when parents want to potty train, especially if there is another baby on the way, but don't rush it. Wait until they're ready – they will be more willing to learn and you won't feel like you're working hard at achieving nothing.

Get them involved. Have your child pick out a special potty and special "big kid" underwear. They will feel more in charge of the situation and will be excited to use their new things.

Use rewards. In the first stages, potty training should be treated like a big deal. Whether it's a small piece of candy every time they use the potty or a larger toy if they can stay dry for a day, provide incentives to the child for being a "big kid." Encourage other family members to talk about how good the child is doing and how great it is that they're learning how to use the potty.

Make a schedule. One of the hardest things for children to master is getting to the bathroom before they go. When you first start training, set a timer to go off every 10 or 15 minutes. When it does, take your child into the bathroom and have them sit on the potty. Not only will this help you avoid accidents, but your child will also learn what it feels like when he has to go.

Be patient. It takes most children weeks or even months to learn to use the potty. Keep at it, stay consistent, and eventually they'll get it.

Milestones

The below milestones are simply guidelines to give you a general idea of what your child should be able to do and can be used to check your child's progress at each stage of development.

But it's important to remember that every child develops differently. Some children will reach milestones early and some will be a little behind. If you are concerned about your child's development, it's important to speak with your child's paediatrician and follow his or her advice.

The following list is adapted from healthychildren.org, from the American Academy of Paediatrics.

As a toddler, your child should be able to:

- Walks alone
- Pulls toys behind when walking
- Begins to run
- Stands on tiptoe
- Kicks a ball
- Imitates behaviour of others
- Aware of herself as separate from others
- Enthusiastic about company of other children
- Finds objects even when hidden 2 or 3 levels deep
- Sorts by shape and colour
- Plays make-believe

As a preschooler, your child should be able to:

- Climbs well

- Walks up and down stairs, alternating feet

- Kicks ball

- Runs easily

- Pedals tricycle

- Bends over without falling

- Imitates adults and playmates

- Show affection for familiar playmates

- Can take turns in games

- Understands "mine" and "his / hers"

- Makes mechanical toys work

- Matches an object in hand to picture in book

- Plays make believe

- Sorts objects by shape and colour

- Completes 3 - 4 piece puzzles

- Understands concept of "two"

Chapter 9

Resources

Part of being an empowered mum is knowing when you need help – and knowing where to look for trusted, accurate information. There is an overwhelming amount of information out there – and you definitely can't trust everything you read on the internet. When you have a serious issue with your child, it is always best to start with your child's doctor. For less serious issues, the internet, friends, and other resources can be a great place to get helpful information. Just be sure to ask people you trust and for anything you aren't sure about, consult a doctor.

I've compiled a list of some of my favourite resources.

Trusted Nanny Services

www.nightnannies.com

www.eden-nannies.co.uk

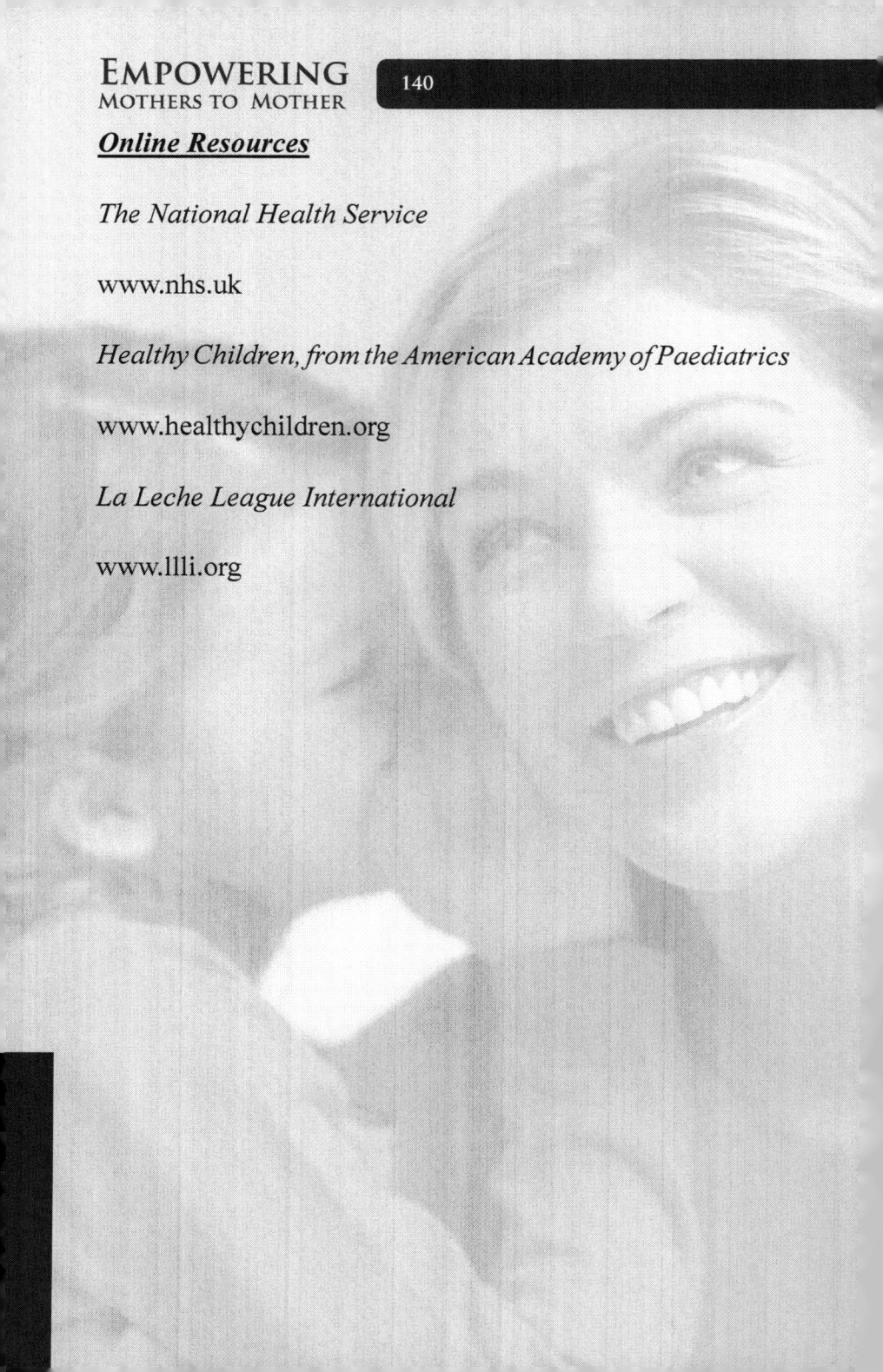

Online Resources

The National Health Service

www.nhs.uk

Healthy Children, from the American Academy of Paediatrics

www.healthychildren.org

La Leche League International

www.llli.org

Checklist for Interviewing Nannies

The following is a list of suggested questions to ask when interviewing nannies:

- ✓ What is your educational background? (Ask for documentation)

- ✓ What experience do you have with babies?

- ✓ What is your strategy for [specify your concerns, i.e., feeding, sleeping through the night, etc.]

- ✓ Will you respect my wishes, even if they aren't the same as your philosophy?

- ✓ It's important to remember that after asking these questions and some of your own, if the candidate looks great on paper but you still feel uncomfortable, take your time making the decision. I have a saying that is "I don't buy stress". I have met many mothers who stress about their nanny and as a result cannot rest because they are always anxious. The nanny is there to help you, not stress you.

Cheat Sheet for Your Village

Use the following sheet to create your own list of information, for each of your children, for those people who may have to take care of your children when you're not available.

Child's Full Name: _____

DOB: _____

Mum's Phone #s: _____

Dad's Phone #s: _____

Doctor's Phone #: _____

Allergies: _____

Medical Conditions: _____

Current medications: _____

Past hospitalizations/treatments: _____

Useful Information for Babysitters/Nannies anyone helping with your children

Personal Information

Home telephone number	
Home address	
Mum's mobile	
Dad's mobile	
Mum's work number	
Dad's work number	
Doctor's number	
Doctor's address	
Dentist's number	

Useful information

Electricity mains	
First aid box	
Local taxi	
Closest hospital with A&E department	
Telephone number	
Closest Paediatric A&E	
Telephone number	
Nearest chemist (opening hours and telephone numbers)	
NHS Direct	
Ambulance	

Emergency and Medical Information

In case of emergency, alternative contact	
Emergency contact's address	
Emergency contact's phone	
Allergies Name _____ Name _____ Name _____	 _____ _____ _____
Medicines that can be given; 1. 2. 3.	Dosage: 1. 2. 3.
Known medical conditions	

Schedule Sheets for New Mums

The following charts will assist new mums in tracking baby's feeding and sleeping schedules.

Breastfeeding

Date: _____

Feeding Time	Length of Feeding	Side of Feeding (Left or Right)

Formula Feeding

Date: _____

Feeding Time	Length of Feeding	# of Ounces

Sleeping

Date: _____

Time	Length of Nap	# Waking Times*

*How many times baby woke up in the course of the nap or during the night.

Date	Time	Feed (breast/ bottle)	Wee	Poo	Sleep	Comments

When Baby is Crying – Mum's Checklist

1. Is baby hungry?

2. Is it wind?

3. Is it nappy change?

4. Is it hot or cold?

5. Is baby ill?

Before you stress or panic, check this list. Even if it isn't something on this list, take a deep breath and try to remain calm. If the crying continues, you can always call the baby's paediatrician. They are there as a resource to you and even if you feel like you're calling constantly – they won't mind! It will be worth it to put your mind at ease.

When to Call the Doctor

One of the most difficult things about being a new parent is dealing with illness and injury. It's sometimes difficult to tell when something is really wrong with your child and when it's just a normal bump or bruise or cold. I strongly encourage you to be in frequent communication with your paediatrician, especially when you suspect something is seriously wrong.

But sometimes it's okay to treat an injury or illness at home. The following list has been adapted from healthychildren. org, from the American Academy of Paediatrics.

Fever

Call your child's doctor right away if your child has a fever and:

- ✓ Looks very ill, is unusually drowsy, or is very fussy

- ✓ Has been in a very hot place, such as an overheated car

- ✓ Has other symptoms, such as a stiff neck, severe headache, severe sore throat, severe ear pain, an unexplained rash, or repeated vomiting or diarrhoea

- ✓ Has immune system problems, such as sickle cell disease or cancer, or is taking steroids

- ✓ Has had a seizure

- ✓ Is younger than 3 months (12 weeks) and has a temperature of 100.4°F (38.0°C) or higher

- ✓ Fever rises above 104°F (40°C) repeatedly for a child of any age

- ✓ Your child still "acts sick" once his fever is brought down.

- ✓ Your child seems to be getting worse.

✓ The fever persists for more than 24 hours in a child younger than 2 years.

✓ The fever persists for more than 3 days (72 hours) in a child 2 years of age or older.

General Illness

If you can tell your child isn't feeling well and is exhibiting any symptoms or illness, call the doctor if your child has the following symptoms:

✓ Vomiting and diarrhoea that last for more than a few hours in a child of any age

✓ Rash, especially if there is also a fever

✓ Any cough or cold that does not get better in several days, or a cold that gets worse and is accompanied by a fever

✓ Ear pain with fever, is unable to sleep or drink, is vomiting, has diarrhoea, or is acting ill

✓ Drainage from an ear

✓ Severe sore throat or problems swallowing

✓ A rectal temperature of 100.4°F (38°C) or higher in a baby younger than 2 months

✓ Fever and repeated vomiting at the same time

- ✓ Blood in the urine

- ✓ Bloody diarrhoea or diarrhoea that will not go away

- ✓ Not drinking for more than 12 hours

Injury

Children are especially accident prone; they're always covered in bumps and bruises. And most of the time, it's not serious, just a normal part of learning to walk or ride a bike. But do contact your doctor if your child exhibits any of the following symptoms immediately following an injury.

- ✓ Cuts that might need stitches

- ✓ Limping or is not able to move an arm or leg

- ✓ Sharp or persistent pains in the abdomen or stomach

- ✓ Pain that gets worse or does not go away after several hours

Emergencies

Unfortunately, many parents will experience an emergency trip to the doctor or hospital. If you're concerned about your child's health, telephone the emergency services by dialling 999 or go directly to the hospital if your child experiences a severe injury or an abrupt change in mood, well-being, or activity.

Further Information

I still work as a night nanny and I love my job! Here are a few references from families I have worked for and which I'd like to share with you.

Reference 1

Winnie is exactly the kind of person that you would be happy to have in your home with your new baby. She is a mother of 4, obviously very nurturing and she was immediately likeable - within minutes of first meeting her, my husband and I felt comfortable and reassured that she was the perfect person to help look after our 3rd baby at nights. She is incredibly professional and so discreet - I never felt like our personal space was compromised.

If you're like me, and like to do things yourself, you'd probably not naturally choose to have a night nurse. However as Ella was our 3rd child, and only 18 months after our 2nd, I reluctantly agreed with my husband to arrange some help.

I thought after having 3 children that I knew all that there is to know but actually, I didn't! Winnie went through my daily routine with me and night timings and helped me understand little Ella's habits and requirements. Her philosophy is simple and with all her advice she was only ever encouraging and gentle. Not once did I feel that she was imposing or critical. She worked closely with my routine and taught me her tricks. Within only a couple of weeks of Winnie's knowledge and encouragement, little Ella slept 12hrs from 7pm and her daily routine was like clockwork - she was only 9 weeks of age and she's still like that 4 weeks later! Winnie didn't stay as long as she was meant to because Ella did so well, but she's always at the end of the phone for any encouragement or help - she's unconditional in her care and I miss seeing her massive smile.

She's a true angel - and I'd almost consider having a 4th so I could see her again!!

Claire Ferrini

Reference 2

Winnie came to us with amazing references and I am so pleased to say she did not disappoint. She has offered us support and help for the first couple of weeks of our life with a second child. Her input and advice has been invaluable. Winnie clearly has a natural talent for calming and soothing babies and she has a wealth of experience in this area.

From the outset, Winnie was able to reassure us and give us the much needed rest we wanted. We were able to hand over full responsibility for the welfare of our newborn in the knowledge that she was in the best of hands. Winnie used various techniques to settle and soothe our very windy newborn and we could fully trust her to differentiate between her cries so that our baby could be brought to mum promptly for feeds. Our newborn has needed an unusual amount of time to be winded and Winnie has been fully dedicated to the cause!

Winnie is extremely personable and was able to fit into our family with complete ease. Aside from her personal and professional experience of dealing with babies, Winnie has attended numerous courses and read a number of books which adds to her portfolio of skills and enables her to truly excel at her profession. We would not hesitate to recommend Winnie to others in the same situation and would be more than happy to speak to future potential clients to provide a telephone reference if required.

Shan and Vim

Reference 3

It's easy to wax lyrical about Winnie. She has a very calm and professional manner that very quickly soothed our fractious sleep-deprived selves. On first meeting, Winnie spent quality time listening to our trials and tribulations about getting our second child, Fred, 6 weeks old, into a feeding and sleeping routine, as well as spending a night observing him first hand. She was then in a position to offer us invaluable advice about how we might improve his routines, always mindful of our preferences and including our experience and ideas. She personalised and adapted her wealth of knowledge to suit Fred and our hopes to combine breastfeeding, with bottle feeding, and the needs and patterns of our first child. Winnie is gentle and encouraging at every turn, aiming to arm and empower parents with knowledge and confidence to look after their babies. She is very practical, a great listener and has boundless positivity. If only we could bottle her karma and approach to babies! For any parents considering hiring Winnie, we can definitely say she will be the game changer in bringing peace and sanity once more into your lives and that of your wee one.

Francesca and Robert Harrison

Reference 4

Winnie was with us a couple of nights a week for August and September 2013.

She cared for my premature newborn son. She was excellent with him, very caring, very knowledgeable, extremely supportive and encouraging to two very exhausted parents! She is friendly and professional, and gave us some really valuable advice on sleep and feeding. I was beyond comfortable leaving her to care for our son. She is absolutely great, I cannot recommend her highly enough.

Seran Glanfield

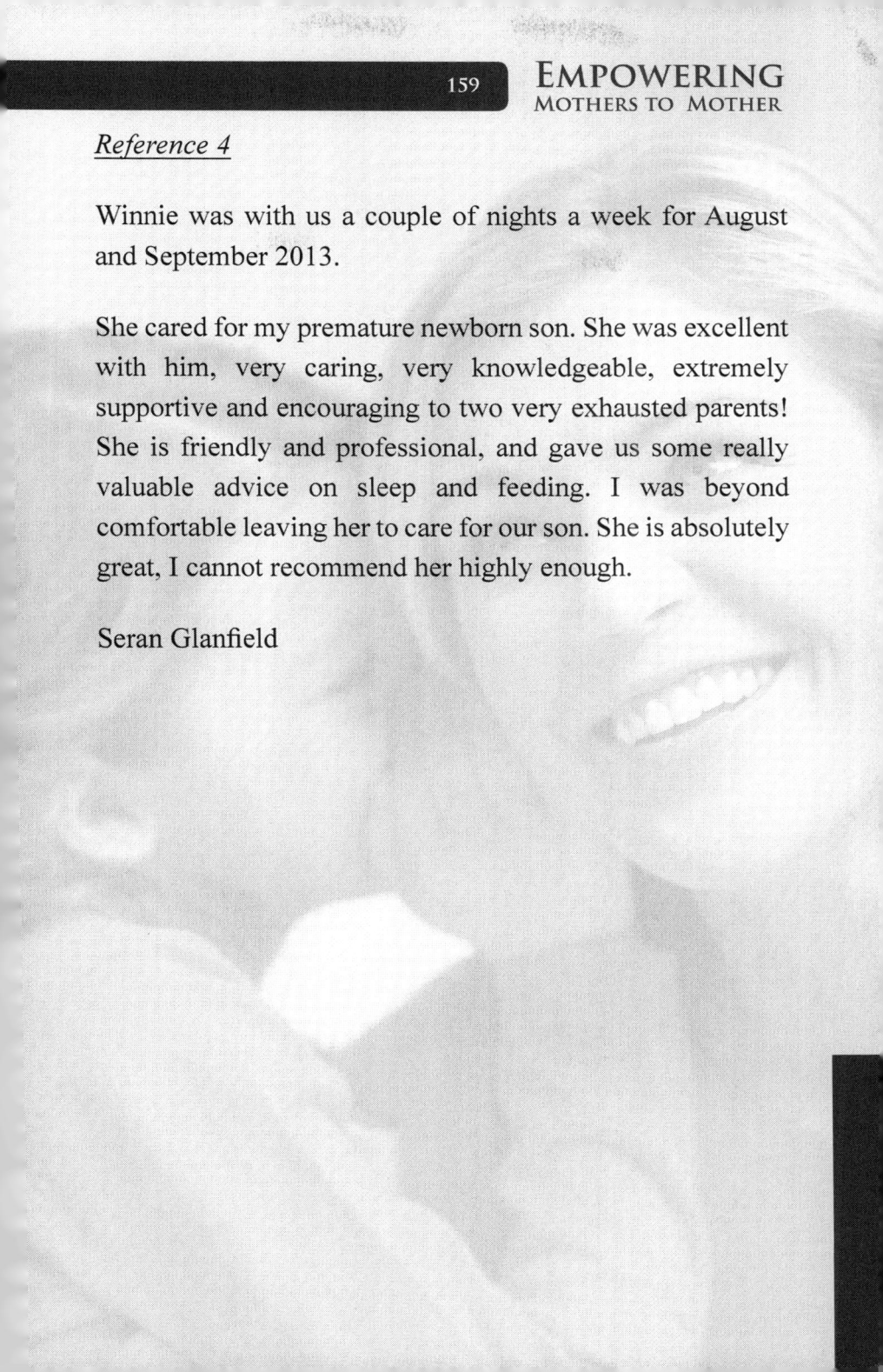

Reference 5

Winnie came to us as a night nurse when our son was 7 weeks old. She has proved to be absolutely brilliant, helping us to not only get my son sleeping through the night, but also weaning him off his dummy, in order for him to settle himself. We are thrilled with the results, and have really enjoyed having Winnie in our home.

She is knowledgeable, friendly and incredibly helpful. She arrives promptly, normally early in order to make sure everything is ready for the night, and we trust her fully. We are able to relax and rest when she is looking after our son, as we know he is in very safe hands.

It has been a pleasure working with Winnie and we will really miss her!

Alexandra Geddes

Reference 6

Winnie Kitaka worked for me as a night nanny for three months, starting immediately after the birth of my third son. The fact that she worked for us for such a long period is a clear indication of how highly we rated her.

Winnie is always smiling, cheerful and has a wonderfully positive attitude and we worked very well together. Her experience as a night nanny and as a mother of three children herself is invaluable. She helped me to guide my son into a good feeding and sleeping pattern, and gave me useful suggestions on how to alter my diet while I was breastfeeding, to aid my son's rather weak digestion. She is a hard worker, dedicated to helping her clients and nothing is too much trouble. I particularly appreciated her putting my second son back to bed when he went for a midnight wander, rather than letting him wake me up when I was so exhausted.

I highly recommend her to any mother.

Sophia Canonaco

Index

=======================================

ONGOING SUPPORT FOR MOTHERS.

If you would like more support from Winnie or to find out
more about her training workshops please go to
www.empoweringformothers.com.

=======================================

Printed in Great Britain
by Amazon.co.uk, Ltd.,
Marston Gate.